PRAISE FOR BILL MYERS

The Jesus
"Myers takes us on an intensely \
He replaces dusty, worn out relig\
friendship with God. This book is \qquad \quad _y who
wants his faith recharged or deepe\
\qquad —Marcus Brotherton, author of *Feast For Thieves*

"Bill Myers reminds us that all we encounter comes from the
hand of an all-wise, all-loving God."
\qquad —Lynn Vincent, coauthor of *Heaven is for Real*

Blood of Heaven
"With the chill of a Robin Cook techno-thriller and the spiritual
depth of a C. S. Lewis allegory, this book is a fast-paced, action-
packed thriller."
\qquad —Angela Hunt, *New York Times* bestselling author

"Enjoyable and provocative. I wish I'd thought of it!"
\qquad —Frank E. Peretti, author of *This Present Darkness*

"The always surprising Myers has written another clever and
provocative tale."
\qquad —*Booklist*

"With this thrilling and ominous tale, Myers continues to shine
brightly in speculative fiction based upon biblical truth. Highly
recommended."
\qquad —*Library Journal*

"Myers weaves a deft, affecting tale."
\qquad —*Publishers Weekly*

The Face of God
"Strong writing, edgy. . . replete with action."
\qquad —*Publishers Weekly*

"If you enjoy white-knuckle, page-turning suspense, with a brilliant blend of cutting-edge apologetics, *The God Hater* will grab you for a long, long time."

—Beverly Lewis, *New York Times* bestselling author

"I've never seen a more powerful and timely illustration of the incarnation. Bill Myers has a way of making the Gospel accessible and relevant to readers of all ages. I highly recommend this book."

—Terri Blackstock, *New York Times* bestselling author

"A brilliant novel that feeds the mind and heart, *The God Hater* belongs at the top of your reading list."

—Angela Hunt, *New York Times* bestselling author

"*The God Hater* is a rare combination that is both entertaining and spiritually provocative. It has a message of deep spiritual significance that is highly relevant for these times."

—Paul Cedar, chairman of Mission America Coalition

"Once again Myers takes us into imaginative and intriguing depths, making us feel, think, and ponder all at the same time. Relevant and entertaining. *The God Hater* is not to be missed.

—James Scott Bell, bestselling author

The Voice
"A crisp, express-train read featuring 3D characters, cinematic settings and action, and, as usual, a premise I wish I'd thought of. Succeeds splendidly! Two thumbs up!"

—Frank E. Peretti, author of *This Present Darkness*

"Nonstop action and a brilliantly crafted young heroine will keep readers engaged as this adventure spins to its thought-provoking conclusion. This book explores the intriguing concept of God's power as not only the creator of the universe, but as its very essence."

—Kris Wilson, *CBA Magazine*

"It's a real 'what if?' book with plenty of thrills. . .that will definitely create questions all the way to its thought-provoking finale. The success of Myers's stories is a sweet combination of a believable story line, intense action, and brilliantly crafted yet flawed characters."

—Dale Lewis, TitleTrakk.com

The Seeing

"Compels the reader to burn through the pages. Cliff-hangers abound and the stakes are raised higher and higher as the story progresses—intense, action-shocking twists!"

—TitleTrakk.com

When the Last Leaf Falls

"A wonderful novella. Any parent will warm to the humorous reminiscences and the loving exasperation of this father for his strong-willed daughter. . . . Compelling characters and fresh, vibrant anecdotes of one family's faith journey."

—*Publishers Weekly*

Imager Chronicles

Myers is our 21st century C. S. Lewis.

—*Light of Life Magazine*

THE JESUS EXPERIENCE

THE JESUS EXPERIENCE

JOURNEY DEEPER INTO THE HEART OF GOD

BILL MYERS

SHILOH RUN PRESS
An Imprint of Barbour Publishing, Inc.

Cover design: Greg Jackson, ThinkPen Design

Published by Shiloh Run Press, an imprint of Barbour Publishing, Inc., P.O. Box 719, Uhrichsville, Ohio 44683, www.shilohrunpress.com

Our mission is to publish and distribute inspirational products offering exceptional value and biblical encouragement to the masses.

Printed in the United States of America.

CONTENTS

INTRODUCTION

Today young adults aren't the only ones fleeing the church and, sadly, in many cases, their faith. I see it happening with seasoned saints and some ministers as well. For some, the pat answers and Bible quotes have become bromides, boring clichés that no longer seem relevant to twenty-first-century life. Others are frustrated at how churches have become museums for the hypocrites instead of hospitals for the broken, or have become fiefdoms of petty power brokers instead of places of truth and grace.

In their commendable efforts to keep the sinking boat afloat, many have amped up their services, either in church or in outside service to others. And it works. . .for a while. But just as surely as the wick in an oil lamp burns itself up if it's not saturated in oil, so believers will burn themselves out with good works if they are not saturated in God. It is the oil of God's presence that should be burning through us, not our good religious works, no matter how lofty.

Trust me, I've been there. It's a vicious cycle of being a Martha servaholic instead of a Mary who "has chosen what is better, and it will not be taken away" (Luke 10:42). In our attempts to be "good Christians," our fruit for God grows smaller and drier until we become exhausted scrub brush, striving to stay alive instead of lush, fruit-bearing trees offering shade to a weary world.

Does this mean we forgo serving others or forget about Christ's great commission to share the Good News? No! On the contrary, it makes the Good News all the better and the success of our efforts all the more powerful.

The truth is: God can do every bit of the work on His own. Initially I hated that idea. It shattered my whole reason for existence (and my secret need to earn God's love and favor). But the fact of the matter is God doesn't need me. Seriously, what can I give Him that He cannot give Himself?

The answer? Nothing.

Well, almost nothing. There is one thing: my friendship. From God's point of view, all my projects, all my service, all my sacrifices are good. But more importantly, they are reasons to be with Him. The works and service are merely Father-son projects, things we can do together as we enjoy each other's company, as we hang with each other, as we love and cry and even joke with one another. That's what God wants. That's what the Creator will not create for Himself—my friendship, my fellowship, my sonship. That's the primary reason I was created. And once I grasped that concept, while falling a dozen times along the way:

- my service no longer became tedious.
- I was no longer frustrated and anxious to reach the end result.
- people were no longer a means to God's end. . .or mine. (This was huge. God's children could no longer be objects I used to earn His approval. Instead they returned to being His children—to be loved and cherished and enjoyed.)

As a result, I am no longer overburdened, overextended, or burned out. The wick of my life is now saturated with

His presence and will burn for a lifetime—and beyond. The paradox is mind-boggling. Now, as I experience the joy of the Lord (*real* joy, not theological comfort), I am more productive than ever. I no longer wake up and sit on the edge of the bed praying, "Oh, Lord, I really need Your help to accomplish Your project today." Now I wake up saying, "Thank You, my Friend, that we have a project to hang out and work on together."

It's the difference between night and day. Between Martha and Mary. Between being an overworked servant with an impossible agenda (but highly esteemed by his fellow overworkers) and a son who basks in the love and friendship of his Father.

That's what I want to share in this book.

How to prevent our faith from drying up. And if it's happening, how to soak in God's presence so His life resumes flowing through us as rivers of *living* water.

It is absolutely possible to return to the excitement and joy we had when we first met Christ. And it is absolutely necessary to replace intellectual philosophy with intimate relationship, to leave being a fearful and dried up servant to become a rejoicing child.

1

↔

IN THE BEGINNING. . .
(OR HOW I GOT INTO THIS MESS)

My earliest memory was sitting on my parents' bed and reading the Bible. Well, maybe not my earliest, and maybe not the whole Bible (hey, I tell stories for a living, so indulge me). But I do remember my dad helping me with the first two words: "In. . .the. . ." I couldn't believe it. I was a genius. I, Billy Myers, could read the Bible!

And it didn't stop there.

For reasons I don't entirely understand, my desire to read scripture continued to grow, even through high school. Seriously, can you imagine a teenage boy eager to get through his homework so he can read the Bible? Of course I didn't tell anybody. After all, I had a reputation to keep up. So while guys my age were busy hiding their *Playboy* magazines, I was busy hiding my Bible.

PULLING OUT ALL THE STOPS

Then came my freshman year at the University of Washington. The girl I had dated through high school dumped me for being a jerk. (No hard feelings, Jan. I wouldn't have dated me in the first place.) So, there I was, doing the mopey, wandering the campus at night with a broken heart thing, when I vowed to give the Lord 100 percent of my life. With the brazen ego only an eighteen-year-old boy could have, I promised I would do whatever He wanted. It didn't matter how stupid it was or how uninformed I thought He might be, I was His man. I would always say yes. I sealed the deal by breaking into the University Presbyterian Church at 2:00 a.m. and doing a little self-baptism. (Don't worry, I got it done right a year or two later.)

And do you know what happened?

Nothing. For about six weeks. And then things got a little interesting.

I was in a theater watching the fourth movie of my life. (Growing up in the foothills of the Cascade Mountains, I didn't get out much.) I had seen *Pollyanna*, *The Parent Trap*, and *Pinocchio*. And now I was watching my fourth movie—*The Godfather*.

I remember my mouth hanging open in shock as people were massacred on the screen. But even more shocking to me were my peers jumping to their feet yelling, "Yeah! Shoot him again! Give it to him! Oh, baby, oh yeah!"

I walked out of that theater absolutely numb. I was amazed at the power of cinema. And since God had apparently not noticed it, I gave Him a detailed briefing: "Did You see what was going on in there? Did You see the way everyone was getting all worked up over all that violence, all that evil? Talk about power! You know what You should do? You should get people to make movies about doing good. Yeah, this is important. You should raise up movie people to do movies that will excite people about good. . . . Hey, maybe even about Yourself!"

But every time I told God what He should do, it seemed

to bounce off Him and come right back at me. This was crazy. I didn't even know how to watch a movie, let alone make one. Most of my life I'd planned to be a dentist. (Only later did I realize that might not have been such a good idea. With my attention deficit disorder, spending three hours in somebody's mouth would not have been so great, as I'd probably start pulling things just to keep it interesting.)

A RADICAL TURN

Anyway, after about six weeks of arguing with God—and being reminded more than I wanted, "Didn't you promise Me you'd do anything I asked?"—I finally cried out, "All right! I'll become a movie whatever-they're-called!" So I changed my major to filmmaking, discovered that the University of Washington didn't have a film department at that time, and wound up at the only film school that would take me—the Italian State Institute of Cinema and Television in Rome. And if you're guessing that would put me in Italy, you'd be right.

Hang on—it gets crazier.

One of the many ways I provide God with amusement is through my learning disability regarding communication. The communication part of my brain is miswired. In fact, I was pretty old as a kid before I ever learned to talk. My folks wondered if I'd ever speak. (And once I started, they wondered if I'd ever shut up.) To get into college, and I'm not proud of this, I had to cheat my way through two years of French. I mean, I could barely speak English, and I was supposed to speak French?

And now, suddenly I was in Rome, Italy, living in a country whose language I can't speak and studying a subject I know nothing about. I was there for an entire year and learned only one phrase: *Dov'è e il bagno?* (Where's the restroom?)—an important phrase to know if you're living in a foreign country for a year.

MORE FOOLISHNESS

Everyone in class thought I was ignorant. Everyone thought I was a fool. And everyone was right. But it sure wasn't boring. Somehow I made it through the program, moved back to Washington, married Brenda, my incredibly patient and loving wife (who didn't pay me to say that), and headed down to Los Angeles to become a rich and famous movie director.

Unfortunately, they already had plenty of those in LA and didn't need any more, so Brenda and I proceeded to do something called. . ."starve." Actually, we didn't starve, but we became experts at eating macaroni and cheese. Honestly, the things you can do with that stuff are amazing. But I digress. Eventually, I managed to get a job directing a stage show—if you count "getting a job" as working for free.

As you might expect, God and I were having some serious heart-to-hearts during this time.

"I don't know what You're doing," I said. "I mean, I promised to do anything You want—well, except write, because I got Cs and Ds in my one writing class in college. And You know that communication problem I have in my brain. But You just name it, and I'll do whatever You want. I'm serious; just tell me and—"

I was interrupted by a phone call from a TV producer. He'd seen the show I was directing and asked if I would consider writing for his TV series. I was stunned. *Me, write? Wasn't God paying attention?* After the initial shock, I asked the producer a very important question at that time in my career: "Do you pay?"

He said, "Oh yes, we pay—"

"You bet!" I interrupted. "I'll be there first thing in the morning!"

Of course, as soon as I hung up, I broke into a panic attack, complete with tears. *What have I done?* I thought. *I don't know how to write! I don't know the first thing about writing.*

FALTERING STEPS

Anyway, long story short, I wrote the worst TV show in history. It was awful. It was so bad that when I watched it, I reached down to the tennis shoe next to the sofa and threw it at the set. And it was my own show! But it paid the bills, and once again I enjoyed the adventure. I was terrible at it. I stunk. But I enjoyed it.

So I wrote a second show. This time the producers were smart enough not to buy it. And a third. Same—no sale. And a fourth. Pretty soon we were back to eating macaroni and cheese until, you guessed it, the phone rang again. This time it was a publishing company back east. They'd heard that there was a "young Christian TV writer living in Hollywood," and if they could just get me to take time out of my busy schedule and write a book for them, they would be so very grateful.

Of course, I asked that all-important question back then: "Do you pay?"

And they gave the all-important answer: "Yes."

"No problem," I replied.

And this time, having previously seen God's mighty hand at work in my life, as soon as I hung up the phone, I broke into another panic attack, complete with tears. "Oh God, what have I done? I know I wrote that TV show, and all those others that no one will buy, but writing a book? Smart people write books. What do I know about writing books?"

And so, I wrote the world's worst book. It was terrible. Awful. And believe me, I have been on eBay, Amazon.com, and every place else I can think of to buy up the last remaining copies so no one can ever find it or will ever know.

But the thing is, I kind of enjoyed writing it. So I wrote another. And for whatever reason, the publisher bought it. And I wrote another, and they bought it, and. . .well, that was 125 books, 8 million books and DVDs sold, and seventy national and international awards ago. I'm hot stuff! Actually, I'm still an imposter; I just haven't bothered to make that public, so let's keep it between ourselves.

KEYS TO SUCCESS

Basically, the keys to my success are:

- I'm a coward.
- I'm a crybaby.
- I'm unqualified

Now that doesn't mean I don't work hard at my craft and try to improve. But when readers or critics gush and I begin to believe my own press, the Lord gives me this little tug on my collar and reminds me of who I really am—a frightened, untalented, mentally challenged child.

But I'm a child who just keeps saying yes.

You see, I learned decades ago that you don't have to be smart. You don't have to be talented. You don't even have to be a very good Christian. (God will take care of that.) But there are so few Christians willing to always say yes to Him that He has to use whoever He can. Sometimes I feel like He's standing in the front of the classroom asking for volunteers as all my peers start examining the tops of their shoes. Meanwhile, I'm in the back, waving my arms and wildly calling out, "Ooo-ooo! Pick me! Pick me!" And since nobody else volunteers, He is resigned to call on me. Honestly, sometimes I feel sorry for Him.

By now, I'm sure some are thinking I'm giving a shuck-and-jive routine, pretending to be Mr. Modest. Well, let's see if I can clear that up with just one of several dozen incidents.

GOD MAKES MORE "MISTAKES"

Many have seen the book and video series I cocreated back in the nineties called *McGee and Me!* It has been aired on networks in eighty countries around the world, including ABC and the BBC and has won a bazillion awards. When it came to Christian kids' videos, we were the talk of the town (till those talking vegetable guys moved in).

And how did you get the job? you're thinking. The same way I've advanced in most everything else—by being a crybaby, a coward, and unqualified but being someone who says yes.

I got a phone call from another uninformed producer.

"Mr. Myers," he said, "we are inviting eighteen of the most creative Christians in the country to the Ritz Carlton at Laguna Beach, California, for three days to create a children's video series. Are you interested?"

Once again, I asked the important question: "Do you pay?"

"Oh yes," he said. "We've got a grant for 1 million dollars."

"I'll be there!"

And when I showed up, I saw that he was right. There were seventeen of the most creative Christians in the country. And then there was me. These guys and gals were so incredibly talented and experienced. One had written for the TV series *Happy Days*. Others had their own production companies. One fellow even claimed to have helped launch singer Amy Grant's career. I was definitely outclassed. And after about forty-five minutes of embarrassing myself, I went up to my room and, being the mighty man of God I'd become, having seen God work miraculously for me time and time again, dropped to my knees and had a good cry.

"Oh, God, what have I done?" I prayed. "I know I promised always to say yes to You, but did You see those people downstairs? I mean, no offense, but You're way over Your head on this one." But being the inventive guy that I am, I came up with a backup plan. "All right," I said. "I'll make You a deal. I have this one lame idea about a kid with a cartoon friend. That's all I've got. I'll share that with the group tomorrow then make up some excuse and say I have to go home early. Deal?"

I waited for an answer. There was none.

"Deal?"

Still no answer. I figured that was as good as yes. Boy, did I have a lot to learn!

The next day I showed up at the meeting and was once again majorly outclassed. Finally, someone turned to me and asked if I had any ideas.

"Yeah," I said. "A kid with a cartoon character friend. Listen, there's an emergency at home and I have to—"

"A cartoon character?" someone responded. "How novel."

"Right," I said, glancing at my watch. "Listen, I have to get going—"

"A boy or girl?"

"A boy?" I half asked. "Listen, I gotta head back—"

"And where does he live?"

After much thought and contemplation, I answered, "A house!" Then, to prove my creative genius, I added, "A *big* house."

And so this continued for two more days. I had no real answers. I just winged it. Until finally, Sunday afternoon, the guy with the check thanked everybody and sent them home—except for me.

"Uh, Bill," he said. "Can you stay after a moment?"

Great, I thought. *I'd been such a slug he was going to make me pay for my room.*

Instead, we went for a walk on the beach, and he said, "Well, I think it's become very clear you are the man God has called to quarterback this project."

Having done some acting during those macaroni and cheese days, I was able to respond appropriately with, "Well, yes, that would make sense. Of course I'm the guy you would choose." Meanwhile, inside I'm screaming to heaven, *What? What are You doing this time? That's a million dollars. Are You paying attention?*

That's how I wound up being the cocreator of *McGee and Me!*—by being a crybaby, a coward, and unqualified, but being somebody willing to say yes even when it made no sense.

Lots of folks have role models from the Bible—Abraham, Moses, Mary, Peter. Do you know who my role model is? Balaam's donkey. That's right. I know if God can use a donkey to speak, then I qualify. So can anybody—if he or she will just say yes.

THE BEGINNING, NOT THE END

So many of my Christian friends see the cross as the end of the line. They believe the salvation experience is their ticket to get into the stadium and sit down to watch the game. But that's not true. The cross is the beginning. It's permission to get onto the field and play the game. Jesus is standing on the 50-yard line, waving for us to come down and play. But we're all so concerned about student loans, our mortgages, or getting our own kids through college that only a handful of us are foolish enough to race down the bleachers and onto the field.

This is what Jesus was talking about when He said, "I've come that you might have life and have it abundantly." It's an adventure, the ride of a lifetime.

Tony Campolo talks about a survey done in nursing homes. They asked residents, "If you could go back in your life and do one thing all over again, what would it be?" One of the top three responses was, "I wish I'd taken more chances."

My whole life is a chance. I don't know what God is going to pull next. I love the line in C. S. Lewis's *The Lion, the Witch, and the Wardrobe* when the children ask if Aslan is safe. "Safe?" Mr. Beaver says. "'Course he isn't safe. But he's good. He's the King, I tell you." Likewise, God isn't always "safe." He challenges us to go beyond what we can do in our own power.

I told Brenda that when I die, I don't want an epitaph on my grave marker. I don't even want a Bible verse. I just want a picture of a man jumping off a cliff screaming, "Here we go again!"

But as exciting as a life of risk taking is, as abundant and fulfilling as it can be, it took me another twenty years to learn that it wasn't enough. It was only a foretaste. And in my single-minded determination always to say yes, to leap on board whenever volunteers were needed, I began depriving myself and my family of the real life God wanted to give us.

Slowly, over the course of two decades, my service to God became my drug of choice. It was a wonderful, intoxicating drug that always *appeared* good and noble and wholesome, but one that threatened all that was important, including my relationship with and my love for Jesus Christ.

2

SEDUCED BY SERVICE

The best thing about getting olde– (ahem) more mature is that you've had a chance to see if all the God stuff folks have been saying to you over the years is actually true.

Well, the reviews are in. And sad to say, at least for me, they're mixed.

The God stuff God says is true. Seriously, I've not caught Him in a single lie, not even an exaggeration. Pretty impressive. But the God stuff some others have fed me over the years is. . .well, for the more delicate sensibilities, let's just call it a load of bovine feces.

In the first chapter, you read about a kid who gave Jesus Christ 100 percent of his life. Now let's talk about what he got wrong and how he found out about it.

GOD WEIGHS IN

I was sitting on the bench in my back orchard, where I spend time with God nearly every morning twelve months out of the year (living in SoCal does have some advantages). It's a quiet place, completely out of view of the neighbors, even from my own house (an important perk for reasons that will soon become apparent). A few years back, I'd brought in a giant dump truck load of sand, added some beach chairs and tiki torches, and made it the perfect spot for the college Bible study I was teaching.

So there I was one morning, minding my own business,

studying the Bible and praying—when suddenly, out of the blue, a thought formed in my head. No, there was no voice, no choir of angels. Not even a burning rosebush. But it was such a strange thought I was pretty sure wasn't my own: *"Son, if I were to put you in a coma and you could not talk to others about Me, could not serve Me in any way, would I be enough for you?"*

I was startled, to say the least. But it seemed just real enough for me to play along—or attempt to. Yet every time I tried to come up with the expected, holy-man-of-God answer, truth kept getting in the way.

I had no other alternative but to go to Plan B: ducking and weaving.

"Too bad about those Dodgers last night," I said. "You ever going to give them a hand in winning?"

"Would I be enough?"

"Right. Listen, You know about my kid's new boyfriend. I really think she could do better. What say You—"

"Would I be enough?"

"Well, will You look at the time. Got that deadline coming up, better get back to work, but thanks for—"

"Would I be enough?"

I tell you, for a random thought, it was pretty persistent. And over the following days and weeks, no matter how hard I tried to drown it out with my busyness or impressive religious service, it just kept coming back. I knew I had to come clean.

I could no longer dodge the question. Finally, I answered,

"So what do You like better, the NIV Bible or the NAS—"

"Would I be enough?"

"All right, all right," I said. Then, after a deep breath, I gave my most honest—and painful—answer: "No, Sir. You would not be enough."

Fortunately, there was no bolt of lightning. No angry earthquake. Not even the stern clearing of an eternal throat. Just the quiet and gentle sense that we were about to begin another adventure.

"But, wait! I already have an adventure! I'm a man on a mission. Remember that promise I made to always say yes to You? Remember how You were going to use me to change the world through movies and media? I've been faithfully following that call for decades. It's all been for You."

It was true. Everything I did was to fulfill that calling—the books, the productions, even mentoring the high school and college kids. It was all about advancing the kingdom of God. The same was true with my inner life. There was no hypocrisy (at least after I was done being a schizophrenic teenager). Everything I thought, everything I did, everything I said was for Him—the service to others, the daily sacrifices of being a good dad and husband, my time studying scripture, my fasting, my prayer life.

GROUND BREAKING—LOTS OF IT

Speaking of prayer, remember that hidden sandlot in my back orchard? Most every night I would spend up to an hour there, pacing and praying, particularly after seeing a questionable TV show or movie.

When it came to prayer, I was a big fan of 2 Kings 13. That's where the prophet Elisha told the king of Israel to strike the ground with a handful of arrows and then he would have victory over the country of Aram. The king took him up on the idea and struck the ground three times. Elisha's reply? "The man of God was angry with him and said, 'You should have struck the ground five or six times; then you would have defeated Aram and completely destroyed it. But now you will defeat it only three times'" (v. 19).

Well that sure wasn't going to be me. I found an old walking stick—actually the broken handle of a garden hoe—and really gave it a workout. At the end of every night, the place looked like a war zone—holes everywhere. The hoe handle didn't last long under that abuse, so I bought another handle, and then another, and. . .well, just between us, the shovel handles at True Value Hardware last the longest.

And didn't I have the success stories to prove it worked?

The answer was often a resounding yes!

But there were other yeses.

Yes, I lived in frustration, and even anger, at the number of nos I received. Yes, more often than not it was exhausting trying to do God's will. (Wasn't He God? Would it kill Him to make things just a little easier?) Yes, I was often frustrated and angry at people for not always catching my vision or, worse yet, blocking me and getting in ~~my~~ God's way.

PEOPLE AS OBJECTS

I had begun seeing people as objects. Hidden underneath my call, my service, my success and failures, I began to view people as tools to advance God's kingdom rather than as children He loved and had died for. They'd become a means to an end. A great end, absolutely, but a means nonetheless.

Equally bad, I began seeing my own life through that same lens. Instead of being God's beloved son and friend, I had become His servant and slave. Without knowing it, I'd downgraded His unlimited love and turned it into something I could earn through hard work and sacrifice. Bottom line: *If I worked harder, maybe I could please Him better.*

Very subtly my purpose in life had become success *for* God instead of intimacy *with* Him.

I had become the Martha in the story of Martha and Mary. I was running around doing important things for Christ, but in the process I was burning myself out—and growing frustrated with those who didn't share my energy.

As Jesus and his disciples were on their way,

he came to a village where a woman named Martha opened her home to him. She had a sister called Mary, who sat at the Lord's feet listening to what he said. But Martha was distracted by all the preparations that had to be made. She came to him and asked, "Lord, don't you care that my sister has left me to do the work by myself? Tell her to help me!"

"Martha, Martha," the Lord answered, "you are worried and upset about many things, but few things are needed—or indeed only one. Mary has chosen what is better, and it will not be taken away from her." (Luke 10:38–42)

Just like Martha, I had become distracted with serving the One I love instead of loving the One I serve. I had lost our friendship. My passion for His ministry had suffocated my passion for His presence. Like the older brother in the parable of the prodigal son, I had forgotten my sonship. And it had taken its toll.

Instead of waking up in the morning and enjoying my time with God and feeling excited to see what He had up His great, cosmic sleeve, I woke up pleading with Him for help to accomplish His projects.

Instead of enjoying life moment by moment, I judged everything and everybody by what they were doing to accomplish God's (and my) agenda. If they came up lacking,

THE JESUS EXPERIENCE — 41

I inwardly considered them a distraction, something to endure and pass as quickly as possible, so I could return to the real, eternal work. I had become so focused on the trophy that I saw the race as a necessary evil to suffer through until I staggered across the finish line.

In short, I had become an excellent slave, a great, efficient gear in what I'd come to see as God's impersonal machine. I had come to love the completed project more than the process.

BUILDING— A VERB, NOT A NOUN

The more I dwelt on the question God had asked me (*"Would I be enough?"*), the more I began to understand that a sovereign God's main purpose for completing a project was *not* to have it completed. If He could create a world in six days, what fraction of a nanosecond would it take for Him to complete my assignments? No, God's main purpose for a building is the actual constructing of that building— *with Him.* His first desire is for it to be a Father-son project, a time for us to enjoy each other's presence, one-on-one. He doesn't *need* my hard work or my skills, He *wants* my companionship.

Isn't that why the Father created us in the first place?

Isn't that why we have children—to enjoy them and for them to enjoy us? I didn't have my children so they could work and slave and build for me. I had them to enjoy their presence and for them to enjoy mine.

So I realized that instead of the toil and labor of constructing a building being the means to an end, it was actually the opposite. It was the day-to-day constructing (the fellowship with Him, the learning to play nicely with others) that *was* the end, that *was* of eternal importance. It wasn't the projects and programs, as important as they may be, but the growth and life that comes from building them.

Yes, realizing that God doesn't need me to accomplish His purposes was a blow to my ego. How could I earn His love? How could I bring down His judgment on those who opposed His righteousness and my God-ordained call? How could I take pride in my accomplishments?

That was a lot for a man on a mission to give up.

But there was something even greater to gain: my growth in sonship. The understanding that as my Father, God wanted me to work beside Him—and He beside me. I didn't have to earn points so He'd like me more. Thanks to Jesus, His love for me was infinite—and how do you add to infinite?

A MAJOR MIND SHIFT

But what about my calling? What about my future programs and past accomplishments?

I soon learned they were merely a carrot on the stick, a reward to draw me into something greater: a deeper relationship with God and with others.

The real purpose in whatever He had me doing was the doing, *not* the being done—the completing, *not* the completed. The eternal goal was the day-to-day hanging out with my Dad at the construction site—and the inevitable transformation that comes from that holy interaction. It was the day-to-day changing of my heart toward Him and toward the community of those working beside me (and, yes, sometimes in opposition to me).

The purpose was not some forgotten sports trophy sitting on a shelf, collecting dust. The purpose was the joy and transformation of a life that comes from playing the game and playing it together.

If I could get hold of that, everything would change. I would no longer see people as objects and tools. Maybe they'd actually start responding to God's love instead of suspecting they were merely cogs in my great plan.

I knew this was the key. If I could love God more than ministry, love His process more than His product, situations would no longer frustrate or discourage me, people would no longer frustrate or discourage me.

God would no longer frustrate or discourage me.

Instead of an obligation, serving God would become a joy. Circumstances would become adventures. And people (including myself) would become something I actually loved.

Okay, that was the truth. Now, how was I to get there? How could I possibly move this from religious theory to flesh-and-bone reality?

3

FALLING BACK IN LOVE

WARNING:

The following account is not the recommended procedure for finding a wife. If used, have the good sense to share it only after you've been married a year or two. (Trust me on this.)

One drizzly Saturday morning at the University of Washington, Tim knocked on my dorm room door. I opened to see him standing in his Fruit of the Looms, smiling like the proverbial cat burping up the proverbial mouthful of feathers.

"I found her," he said.

"Found who?"

"Your wife."

"I'm sorry, *what?*"

"Remember the list you made of all the things you were looking for in a wife?"

"Right."

"I found her."

I quickly ushered him in, throwing a look up and down the hall before shutting the door.

A few months earlier, I had made a list of twenty things I wanted in a wife and passed it out to the guys on my dorm floor. My reasoning was simple: fifty-six testosterone-laden boys could meet a lot more girls than one lone me. Let's face it—if they did their testosterone-laden thing—circulating and going to parties and what-not, while keeping an eye open for me, the odds of finding the right person were much, much better. (I was decades ahead of online dating services.)

So there we sat in my dorm room, going down the list, and lo and behold, she qualified. She passed nineteen points of my twenty-point criteria. The next step was simple: Tim set us up as a blind double date for that evening and—*voila!*—the rest was history—except for the falling in love part.

And that's the point of this little confession: even though we were the right fit for one another, we still had to fall in love. And that didn't happen through lists—or through a clever, albeit slightly strange, young man playing the odds in finding his mate.

It happened through communication. Brenda would talk and I'd listen. I'd talk and Brenda would listen. And eventually, as we got to know each other, it happened. Not overnight, but it happened. (So far so good—we just celebrated our fortieth wedding anniversary and are going for another forty.)

So, is falling in love with God any different? I don't think so. Even though we may know in our heads that He's the perfect intellectual, theological, and philosophical fit, there's still that elusive love factor. And that's what He wants from us. Jesus said to "love the Lord your God with all your heart and with all your soul and with all your mind" (Matthew 22:37).

My point is this: no matter how perfect someone may

be, we can't fall in love with that person if we don't know them. So how do we get to know God? The same way we get to know any other person—through communication; through listening and talking.

STEP 1: LISTENING

Although I have friends who say they literally get audible words from the Lord, I'm pretty much deaf in that department. But I do have His written Word, which by itself is pretty powerful. Remember, it was His Word He used to create the universe, not some advanced course in astrophysics, not some cosmic chemistry set, but His Holy Word.

"God said. . . And it was very good" (Genesis 1). But He didn't stop talking there. We have sixty-six books of scripture. And according to the Bible, "all Scripture is inspired by God" (2 Timothy 3:16 NASB).

Note that it doesn't say *some* scripture or *most* scripture but _all_ scripture. And by "inspired," we're not talking about people getting all excited and worked up about God and then going off to make up fancy fairy tales. The New International Version better translates the New American Standard Bible "inspired" as "God-breathed." This means that somehow, some way, all the words in scripture have the supernatural presence of God infused into them. Somehow they embody His very breath.

And it's not just ultraconservative crazies who think this—unless you want to put Jesus in that boat. He quoted scripture all the time. And He did more than that. Remember in Matthew 4, when Jesus and the devil duked it out in the wilderness? When the devil tempted Him, it's interesting that they didn't fight with swords, smart bombs, or nuclear weapons. Instead, the Creator of the universe and the most evil force in the universe chose to fight with what they knew to be the most powerful weapon in the universe: the Holy Word of God.

Satan would come at Jesus with a quote, and Jesus would counter with another, and on and on they went, fighting only with the power of God's Word.

I accidentally stumbled on this power in my early twenties, when I was involved in the one and only exorcism (or deliverance, or whatever they're calling it these days) I've ever been a part of.

Long story short: a top psychic in LA got my phone number in a dream. He called me, pleading for help, and eventually I wound up in his living room praying for him. I knew nothing about deliverance from evil spirits, except for what Jesus and the boys did in the Bible. But what I did know seemed to work pretty well—except for the time frame. The man had more than a dozen of the things inside him. And thinking I could deal with only one at a time, I turned it into a long, drawn-out affair. Poor man.

As time dragged on, I grew tired, and quite frankly, I

was running out of things to pray. So I opened my Bible and read a short piece from one of the Psalms. Talk about hitting a nerve! The things inside him went ballistic, causing him to writhe, squirm, and shout more R-rated language than a Scorsese movie.

Of course, I thought that was pretty strange, and I tried it again.

Again, he went through the same screaming contortions.

It was an interesting phenomenon, to say the least. I'm not sure it speeded up the process, but whenever I got tired or a little cranky, I'd open the Bible and read something just to stir things up. Immature on my part? You bet. Did it give me a greater respect for the Word? A lot.

(If you're interested, I wrote a detailed and somewhat humorous account of that time in a little e-book titled *Supernatural War*, available on Amazon.com.) Remember in Ephesians 6:13–17, where we're told to put on the full armor of God? It's worth noting that of all the articles of war mentioned, only one is an offensive weapon: "The sword of the Spirit, which is the word of God" (v. 17).

Not only is the Word a weapon, but it is a great surgical instrument in the hands of the Great Surgeon: "For the word of God is alive and active. Sharper than any double-edged sword, it penetrates even to dividing soul and spirit, joints and marrow; it judges the thoughts and attitudes of the heart" (Hebrews 4:12).

But its power lies in more than just being a weapon. Here are a handful of other attributes of God's Word:

- It cleanses us (Ephesians 5:26).
- It equips us to do good works (2 Timothy 3:17).
- It gives us faith (Romans 10:17).
- It allows us to see our real selves (James 1:23–25).

QUALITY, NOT QUANTITY

Listening to God through His Word is more than knowing and quoting Bible verses. Far too many Christians know the Word of God without knowing the ultimate Word, Jesus Christ (John 1:1). They know *about* Him, but they don't *know* Him. They haven't tasted Him, they haven't drunk Him, they haven't eaten and ingested Him into their souls.

Let's face it, you can collect all the maps of Paris you want, but it's a far cry from actually visiting Paris or, better yet, living there. The same is true with the Word. Many have studied the maps of God but haven't lived in Him or let Him live in them.

In today's lightning-fast world, it's easy to blast through a Bible chapter (or chapters, if you're cramming them into a one-year reading program) so quickly that we simply skim across its surface without ever allowing it to enter our souls.

That's where a technique old-timers used comes in handy. It's called *lectio divina* (Latin for "divine reading"). Wikipedia describes it as "a practice of scriptural reading, meditation, and prayer intended to promote communion with God. . . . It does not treat scripture as texts to be studied but as the Living Word."

Lectio divina became a popular way of reading scripture for people as early as the third century. And for me, it's the difference between night and day. Instead of speed reading and getting as much information as possible as quickly as possible, I read one verse or paragraph very slowly, sometimes out loud. I chew on it, savor it, mediate on it. And most importantly, I ask the Holy Spirit (whose job it is to instruct and counsel) to teach me and reveal how the Word's truth applies specifically to me.

As I meditate on the verse or verses, their truths start to impact me, resonate with me, and become a part of me—in a sense, God's Word starts to become my flesh. As I take the time to digest the Word, it grows from intellectual fact into a living, transforming presence within my soul.

BE STILL AND KNOW. . .

God most often speaks in a still, small voice. He seldom shouts or stomps His foot, demanding our attention. He doesn't scream over our blaring music, our loud parties, or our adrenalin-pumping movies. Instead, His voice, which often comes as a gentle impression, is usually very soft—a quiet whisper that is easy to miss in our media-saturated, speed-of-light lives.

That's why I've carved this verse into the table where I have my morning time with God: "Be still, and know that I am God" (Psalm 46:10).

Do I want to know God? I mean *really* know Him so I can *really* love Him? Then I need to be still and dwell on Him.

Was it hard for me to learn this discipline? Did I mention my work is in the entertainment industry? Did I mention my ADD? Did I mention I'm president of a film company?

But as I sit there each morning, forcing my soul to be quiet, I gradually begin to sense the peace of His presence, the peace of trusting Him, the peace of knowing His great love for me: "Peace I leave with you; my peace I give you. I do not give to you as the world gives" (John 14:27).

But what about my call to change the world? I want Him to be exalted, but how can I do that by being still and just watching and listening as valuable time slips away? I suspect His response is, "How can you accomplish those things if you don't spend time with Me?" Or, to quote Him more accurately: "If you remain in me and my words remain in you, ask whatever you wish, and it will be done for you" (John 15:7).

Not long after I carved the verse about being still into my table, I noticed it actually had a second part I had never read before: "I will be exalted among the nations, I will be exalted in the earth." So, in its entirety, the verse reads: "Be still, and know that I am God; I will be exalted among the nations, I will be exalted in the earth" (Psalm 46:10).

What? Really? If I want to exalt God among the nations, I'm supposed to just be still and know Him? What a strange, wonderful, paradox!

So today as I quiet my soul and dwell on Him, I see Him more clearly. And as I see Him more clearly, I realize He has the sovereignty thing all locked up. He's totally in control. He'll do all the heavy lifting.

And my job? Be still and know He is God.

And it's not just for my early morning times. As I fight SoCal traffic every day, I purposely turn off my radio and my iwhatever and simply enjoy the silence—His silence and His peace. The same thing goes for my work. If I begin feeling overwhelmed on a movie set or at a meeting, I just slip off for twenty minutes to be still.

As a word of caution, there's more to meditation than just being still. This is no Eastern religious exercise. It's being still *and* knowing He is God. Instead of emptying my mind, I'm being filled with God.

STEP 2: TALKING

The second part of communicating and falling in love is talking —no great revelation there. And it's also no great revelation that talking to God involves praying. Of course the perfect model for prayer is the one Christ gave us:

> *"And when you pray, do not keep on babbling like pagans, for they think they will be heard because of their many words. Do not be like them, for your Father knows what you need before you ask him. This, then, is how you should pray: 'Our Father in heaven, hallowed be your name, your kingdom come, your will be done on earth as it is in heaven. Give us today our daily bread. Forgive us our debts, as we also have forgiven our debtors. And lead us not into temptation, but deliver us from the evil one.' "*
> (Matthew 6:7–13)

For starters, check out the intimacy He insists already exists in this prayer. Jesus tells us that instead of babbling and thinking we can wear out some unfeeling God with an overabundance of words, we're to call God our Father and understand that He already knows what we need. He tells us that instead of begging and pleading, we're to enter into a Father-child conversation.

In fact, the very first words of the prayer are an acknowledgment of that relationship. It's not, "O mighty God or "O great and powerful One who can squash me like an ant." Instead, it's two words: "Our Father" (some say a better translation is "Our Daddy," "Our Papa," or "Our Dad"). This clearly sets the tone for heart-to-heart communication between a trusting child and a tenderhearted Parent (who just happens to be in heaven running the entire universe).

But look what's next. No begging, no pleading. Just love and praise: "Hallowed be your name."

Over the years, I've learned to begin my time with God this way. First and foremost, I remind myself, and the rest of creation, how awesome He really is—which is probably why scripture says that's how we are to approach Him: "Enter his gates with thanksgiving and his courts with praise; give thanks to him and praise his name" (Psalm 100:4).

Praise isn't some grand kiss-up formula for buttering God up so I can manipulate Him into doing what I want Him to do. It's merely proclaiming truth to all who are listening, including myself.

Prayer doesn't necessarily exclude petitioning God. Jesus certainly includes that in His model prayer as well. Yet I'm often perfectly content simply to stay with praise and adoration, thanking Him for who He is and for what He's done in my life.

To be honest, I'm amazed at how unappreciative I can be—how I can whine and complain over a broken nail when I should be thanking God for my entire hand. So on those grumpy, self-pitying days, I force myself to thank Him for something, anything—even "inconsequential" things like the color blue, the dew on a spiderweb, or the intricate latticework in a decaying leaf. And as I tell my emotions to take a backseat and I focus on the real truth of who God is and what He has done in my life (much like David practiced in many of his psalms), I eventually start to feel His peace and love. As that happens, I can't help but love Him back.

God's love is radioactive. Simply by basking in it, I begin glowing with it. And when I direct it back to Him, He directs it back to me with interest, which I direct back to Him, which he directs back with more interest—and on and on it goes and grows. It's like a game of Who Can Outgive Whom. And the cool thing is, God never loses. He can't help Himself. Winning is His nature. And the more He wins, the more I'm blessed.

SOBBING IS GOOD, TOO

There have been times in my life when I've been so overcome with pain or grief that I've stripped down, stepped into our shower, and sat curled up on the floor, letting the water pound on me as I wept (my twenty-first-century version of sackcloth and ashes). Of course I knew God was in charge, but I've learned that it doesn't hurt to occasionally run to Him like a little child with our heartache and cry, "Daddy, it hurts! Please make it stop." He gets that. More than once, Jesus shed tears over other people's pain and plight—even when, as with Lazarus, He was about to provide the miraculous solution.

Instead of plastering on a pious, it's-all-good smile, I've found that by sharing my deepest hurts and deepest disappointments—yes, even my disappointments with God Himself—I've created a much stronger and more honest bond of love with Him.

SLOW DANCING WITH GOD

In learning to love God, my imagination also comes in handy. I know that as long as I'm imagining what scripture has already verified as true, I'm on safe ground.

We'll discuss this later, but at least eighteen times the Bible, in one sense or another, refers to us as Christ's bride. Not His old lady, not His ball and chain, not even His wife—but His bride.

That means Christ loves me with the same passion a bridegroom has for his bride on their wedding night. In fact, I tell those I mentor that when they go to a wedding, yes, make a big deal about the bride walking down the aisle (and the dress that cost her dad way too much money). But also sneak a peek back at the groom. Take a look at his face and know those feelings of love and compassion are what Christ feels for them every millisecond of our lives.

Is that intense? Yes, but it's absolutely true.

Is it hard to always see or feel? Yes, but it's absolutely true.

That's where faith comes in.

And imagination. Granted, it may be easier for someone like myself, who makes his living with his imagination. But imagining God's love when I can't see it is a close cousin to having faith in that love. In fact (and don't let this get around), but remember that secluded sandlot I used to beat up with my staff/True Value Hardware shovel handle in prayer in Chapter Two? Well I still go down there, but instead of pacing around angry, pounding the ground with it in prayer, I slip in my ear buds, play a special slow song that expresses my love for God, close my eyes, and in my imagination slow dance with Him.

So, at least for me, finding ways to use my imagination to grasp the scriptural truths of God's great love has been helpful.

ONE FINAL THING

Do you want to know God better and love Him more? Then ask Him for help.

I can't think of any prayer God would rather answer than, "Please, Jesus, help me love You more." It resonates much the same way as the prayer of the man in Mark 9:24, who cried out to Jesus, "I do believe; help me overcome my unbelief!"

God really gets behind that type of honesty because He doesn't have to waste time tearing down hypocritical, religious nonsense. No demolition of false foundations is necessary. He can immediately begin building on that bedrock of truth as He continues embracing and shaping His sons and daughters into all He made us to be.

In closing, pursue loving God. We'll talk about works and service in an upcoming chapter, but keep in mind that the Great Commandment, "Love the Lord with all your heart, soul, mind and strength," trumps the Great Commission. There is absolutely nothing more important than falling more and more deeply in love with God.

As I pursue that love and allow it to capture me, Christianity becomes less of a religion and more of a relationship, and Jesus Christ becomes less of a historical figure and more my good Friend. Every day as I pursue the love of Jesus Christ, He becomes less of a philosophy and more the intimate Lover of my soul.

4

THREE CORNERSTONES

Back in the days when Christians inside the Soviet Union (now Russia) were persecuted by their own government, I directed some films for an organization smuggling Bibles into the country. I was researching a project inside the borders, and my interpreter and I pretended to be tourists by day then sneaked off to meet high-level, persecuted Christians by night. It was mid-January and so cold at night that the wind chill brought the temperature down to minus seventy degrees. I still have the tiniest trace of frostbite on one ear to prove it.

We'd been preparing for days for one rendezvous, and that included blending in with the people so the KGB would not follow us. This meant buying Russian clothes, which included those thick fur hats everyone wears there. Once we were sure we passed as Russians, we hit the streets. It was an arduous task of heading up one avenue for several blocks, then turning and backtracking down that same street. Then up another avenue and turning and backtracking—all the time keeping a careful eye out to make sure we were not being followed.

It was hard, cold, and grueling, but a small part of me also thought it was pretty cool. All right, a *big* part of me. I could already envision the title of my biography: *Bill Myers, Secret Agent for God.*

After several hours of this, once my interpreter was certain we were "clean," we made our move. But we'd no sooner headed for the designated bus stop to board and travel another hour through the city and suburbs than a jolly citizen (an oxymoron for any Russian on the streets in the dead of winter) cried out, "Americans! Americans!"

We slowed to a stop, our cover blown.

"Americans, wait up! Americans!"

He loudly chattered away as he approached us. As the self-appointed welcoming committee, he drew all sorts of attention. He even gave us dove lapel pins (which I have on my bulletin board to this day) that said to us, *We shall be forever friends!*

"Yeah, da, da," my guide said as he glanced up and down the street, realizing there was no way we could continue our mission.

Finally, I asked, "How did you know?"

"Know what, my good friend?"

I motioned to our clothes. "We were trying to fit in. How could you tell we were American?"

"Ah, such a thing, it is very easy." Without a word, he reached up to my cool fur hat, turned it around, and set it back on my head. "To fit in, it is best not to wear your hat backwards!"

We all had a good laugh—or pretended to. When we'd finally said our good-byes (and I no longer looked like an idiot), we began the procedure all over again. Up a street and down a street, up a street and down a street.

Three hours later, we sat in a devout brother's tiny apartment sharing the story and having another good chuckle.

But as things grew serious, our host began sharing the difficulties he and his family had endured because of their faith in Jesus Christ.

My heart really ached for him, and as we finally broke up, I said through my interpreter, "Brother, I want you to know I'll be praying for you."

He just looked at me sadly and shook his head. "No," he said. "We are the ones praying for you."

I frowned. "What do you mean?"

"We have our trials, which make us stronger. But you in the West, you have no such things, so you are growing weaker every day. It is for *your* faith that we pray."

His words irritated me at first. What about all those parties I don't get invited to? What about those studio execs who don't return my calls? What about the AC that's out in my car? But the more I thought of his version of persecution versus mine, the more he made sense.

I received a refresher course soon after this in China. Remember the attack on the college students in Tiananmen Square in 1989—particularly the photo of the student standing defiantly in front of an army tank? As that unrest continued, I stole into the country to research a film I would direct dealing with the plight of the underground church in China. During that time, I spoke to several Christians who had been imprisoned for their faith—a faith that seemed only to grow stronger and more determined.

The reason for their strong and growing faith? Their trials and hardships.

That's not to belittle the trials we face in the West. Somehow they still find their way to us. They may be different, but just as devastating. The heart-wrenching divorce that can be worse than death because the corpse is still alive. Children we've sacrificed and would die for who are bent on destroying themselves. Disease that slowly ravages and sucks out the life of those dearest to us. Anybody from any culture who says Christians are exempt from such suffering is simply lying. In some ways, it can seem even more painful for Believers because we know there is a God in control who could stop the pain any time He wanted.

Over the years, I've come to embrace three scriptures as the cornerstone to my walk with God. (Can a person have three cornerstones? What do I know? I'm an artist, not an architect.) Each one by itself was pretty profound, but when all three came together, they radically altered my understanding of my life in Jesus Christ.

CORNERSTONE 1: KNOWING THAT GOD BRINGS GOOD FROM ALL THINGS

And we know that in all things God works for the good of those who love him, who have been called according to his purpose. (Romans 8:28)

I know, I know—this is a verse lots of folks probably

memorized back in Sunday school. For many, it's nothing more than a religious cliché, a bromide to rattle off whenever things get tough. But the first time I heard it, it stopped me dead in my tracks. *Seriously*, I thought, *has anybody paid attention to the words? I mean* really *paid attention?*

"In *all* things God works for the good?" Are you kidding me? At first I thought it was a typo. Surely the author meant "in *some* things," or, giving him the benefit of the doubt, "in *most* things." But in every Bible I checked, the same word came up: *all*.

You mean to tell me if my dog runs onto the freeway, loses a game of "tag" with a semitruck, and winds up in puppy heaven, that if I love God and am called according to His purpose, it's supposed to work together for my good?

Or, raising the stakes much higher, are you telling me that if my daughter comes down with some disease that puts her in excruciating pain, and I can only sit there and watch her writhe, that it's supposed to work together for my good? For hers?

Don't get me wrong, I buy Jesus Christ dying on the cross. And I'm a big fan of Him rising from the dead. But this?

Still, if I chose to believe the whole Bible was the Word of God (and not a buffet line of verses I could pick and choose from), then I had to accept the whole package. And the whole package said that if I loved God and was doing what He wanted, everything would somehow, someway work together for my ultimate good—*everything*.

When I finally accepted that this might be true, I began looking at every event, good or bad, as something God used for my good. No easy task, but that perception gradually began to overhaul my outlook on life. Instead of falling into a woe-is-me victim mentality, I began looking at how I could use even the ugliest of circumstances for my own good.

In some martial arts, like judo, the trick is to use your opponent's attacking force against him. If he lunges at you, pull him even farther forward, throw him off balance, and drag him to the floor. I've seen that happen dozens of times in my life when things go bad or when I feel I'm under attack. It's gotten to the point that I seriously look for God's brightest victories in the darkest places.

This certainly seems the pattern with people in the Bible. We see it with Joseph when his brothers betrayed him. It doesn't get any darker than to have your own flesh and blood sell you into slavery. We see it with Abraham. It doesn't get any darker than having to sacrifice your one and only son. And we see it with Jesus on the cross. It doesn't get any darker than being cut off from your Father, suffering an excruciating death, and taking on the punishment of sin for the entire world.

But through the darkness of his brothers' betrayal, Joseph rose up to become not only ruler over his brothers, but the second most powerful man in the world. Through the darkness of God's testing, Abraham became the father of not just one child, but of many nations. And through the darkness of the cross, Christ saved an entire world (then returned to His position as Ruler of the universe).

The pattern of how God works through even the worst of circumstances is as obvious as it is impressive.

WHO WANTS HAM?

I was thinking of this very pattern during one of my own encounters with darkness. It was forty-eight hours before we were to begin filming a project in Hong Kong. We'd spent tens of thousands of dollars scouting and signing up our Asian cast and crew. We were ready to go.

Well, not quite.

At the second to last production meeting, my Asian producer said, "Mr. Myers, we have just one last issue."

"What's that?" I asked.

"As the director, on the first day of filming you will be required to burn incense and sacrifice a pig to our local gods."

I looked at her and blinked. "You're kidding, right?"

"No, Mr. Myers. We are quite serious. If you do not perform this ceremony, the cast and crew will not work for you."

"Why not?"

"You Westerners, in your arrogance, trample all over our gods and beliefs. As a result, during the filming, someone is almost always hurt or killed." She gave a tenuous smile. "I, of course, do not believe such things, but many of your cast and crew do."

I swallowed hard then explained that as a Christian, I could not do this in good conscience. Then I tried to diffuse the situation with my stellar humor, saying something about having a pig barbecue. I wasn't sure she bought it. The following day, I was certain she didn't.

Twenty-four hours before we were scheduled to begin rolling, we sat around the preproduction table for our last meeting. Every department head was there—wardrobe, makeup, transportation, camera, sound. We were just wrapping up the meeting when my producer said, "By the way, regarding the matter of the pig sacrifice?"

The room grew silent. I glanced around at some very serious faces. Apparently, word had spread. I cleared my throat. "I'm sorry," I said, "I thought I'd made that clear. As a Christian, that's not something I can do."

"And that is okay," my producer said. "Because we have found a solution. You will not have to do such a thing."

I breathed a sigh of relief. "That's great."

"Instead, your assistant director will perform the ceremony."

So much for relief. I glanced back around the table. Everyone nodded in satisfaction—everyone but me. It made no difference to me who performed the sacrifice, the principle was the same. As the leader, I would still be responsible.

Talk about being in a jam. If I said yes, I'd not only betray my faith but be dedicating the film to other "gods." If I said no, I'd come off even more inflexible than the day before, and my cast and crew would walk. All the money we'd spent in preproduction would be lost. The film would be over before it started.

But how could I say yes?

I stared down at the table, not even having the courage to look anyone in the eye. I wish I could say I answered in the powerful, "No! Thus saith the Lord," voice of Elijah. I did manage to say no, but it came out squeaking more like Pee-wee Herman than Elijah.

After I took my stand (and remained staring at the table), I heard feet shuffling. I knew they were exchanging looks, wondering if they should be calling their agents to line up another job. I also remember silently praying, *Listen, God. . .about victory hiding in darkest places? Well, it doesn't get any darker than this. If You have any suggestions, I'm all ears.*

And then, "out of the blue," a thought came to mind. It wasn't much, but it was all I had.

I looked up and said, "First of all, you need to know, I don't doubt these gods you're afraid of exist. And I believe the deaths and injuries you've mentioned can happen. But as a believer in Christ, I have a different name for those gods. We call them [insert gulp here] demons."

So much for diplomacy. I pushed on.

"But you folks, you believe Jesus Christ is at least a god, don't you?"

They began to nod. "Oh yes. Absolutely. One of the top ten. Yes, a great god."

"And if push came to shove, He could probably take on those smaller gods you're so worried about?"

"Oh yes. He is a most powerful god."

"Well, me and Him, we're pretty tight. What if, instead of offering a prayer to those little gods we know He could beat, what if I offered a prayer of protection to Jesus, instead?"

I saw the crack of light and pushed on. "Better yet, why don't we do it together every day. . . . You know, just to be safe?"

Ever so slowly, they began to nod.

For the record, I never force a secular crew to pray with me. But these folks wanted to. So every day before filming, I led forty non-Christians in a prayer asking for the Lord's blessings and protection. "And, oh yeah, Jesus, if there's anyone here whom You'd like to have put their faith in You, please help them." (You can take the evangelical out of the director, but you can't take the director out of the evangelical.)

The results? No one was killed. Not a single person was injured. And at least two actors, along with their families, put their faith in Jesus Christ. It's also the most powerful film I've directed. I recently spoke to a missionary from South America who said he's still showing the film, and after twenty-five years, it's still bearing fruit.

Why? Because I'm such a genius director? Pretty doubtful. It was because I managed to take God at His Word, because I believed "all things work together for the good." And most importantly, because I pressed in, going all the way.

But that's only the first foundation stone. There are two more.

CORNERSTONE 2: REJOICING IN THE MIDST OF TRIALS

> *Consider it pure joy, my brothers and sisters,*
> *whenever you face trials of many kinds,*
> *because you know that the testing of your faith*
> *develops perseverance. Let perseverance finish its*
> *work so that you may be mature and complete,*
> *not lacking anything.* (James 1:2–4)

What? Another over-the-top adjective? *Pure* joy? Obviously, *this* was a typo. Surely, it was supposed to be *some* joy, or maybe, *mostly* joy.

But *pure* joy?

To make matters worse, this verse was written by James, the fellow leading the Jerusalem church at a time when Christians were being slaughtered and persecuted in droves. To them, he dared write, "*pure* joy"? Was he trying to put a good face on a terrible situation, or, like my persecuted brothers and sisters in Russia and China, was he sharing something deeper?

There's an old story about a restaurant that opened in San Francisco when the city was first getting started. The patrons, many of whom were from the East Coast, wanted the restaurant to serve North Atlantic cod. Happy to oblige, the restaurant purchased the fish from some East Coast fishermen, who cleaned it and packed it in ice, then sent it by boat to San Francisco. But because of the lengthy shipping time, by the time the delicacy arrived, it was anything but fresh.

No problem. They decided to put the fish into open barrels and ship them live. But over the weeks of lounging around in the barrels, the living fish lost all tone and firmness, leaving the flesh soft and pasty.

Now what?

Finally, someone remembered the tenacious personality of catfish and that they were natural enemies of the cod. So they put the cod into the barrels as before, but this time they dropped in one or two catfish to chase them round and round the barrels the entire time they were being shipped.

The result? Firm, fresh, tasty cod—as good as back home.

So if I combine James' statement with Romans 8:28, then maybe I really should "consider it *pure* joy whenever I face trials" because "*all* things work together for my good," with the final purpose that, I "may be mature and complete, not lacking anything."

What a plan!

By combining these two truths, I realized that God was on my side in every situation. I could envision Him as my personal trainer who would take anything thrown at me, turn it around, and use it to make me "mature and complete." All I had to do was stay with the program and consider it "pure joy."

When I was in high school, I was captain of my high school tennis team. (No big accomplishment; my school was so small that if you owned a racket and a pair of tennis shoes, chances were you'd make varsity.) My grandma lived one block way from the school, and she made great chocolate chip cookies. So on the days when the coach said, "Okay Myers, take the team on a run around the town," I was only too happy to oblige.

We'd start off running, disappear around the block, and drop by Grandma's, where we sat around drinking milk and eating cookies. Then, at the appropriate time, we said our good-byes, splashed water on our faces, and staggered back to the school pretending we were exhausted. It didn't happen often, but when it did, everyone was happy. The coach got to go get some coffee, and we got to lounge around drinking milk and eating cookies. A definite win-win.

Well, not quite. For some reason, our team lost every match that year. We just didn't seem to have the stamina or skills of the other teams.

Scripture is pretty clear that God is not the author of

difficulties, but it is equally clear that He is sovereign and will use difficulties for our good. Or, as my dad used to say, "Son, every kick in the butt by the devil just lifts you closer to heaven."

I think this also explains why God is not real keen on answering the "why" questions.

"God," we shout as we stomp our feet, "I demand to know why You're doing this to me." We seem to forget that the entire book of Job deals with that very question. And no matter what Job said or did, he never got an answer from God—just a stern, throat-clearing reminder of his place on the cosmic food chain.

Folks who demand that the God of the universe justify Himself to them are like people standing in the middle of railroad tracks demanding that an oncoming freight train stop and explain itself. Good luck with that!

From scripture, and from my own experiences, I see that God seldom answers *why*.

But He does answer *how*.

How can I cooperate with Him in what is happening?

How can I learn from this trial?

One approach yells and even rebels against God for what is going on. The other believes He always tells the truth and will do its best to cooperate with Him in accomplishing that ultimate purpose of being "mature and complete, not lacking anything."

Just for the record, the Apostle Paul says we suffer for three reasons:

1. Disobedience. If someone sleeps around and comes down with an STD, it's pretty tough to pin that one on God.

2. As we've just read in James, trials make us mature and lacking nothing.

3. Suffering enables us to comfort those who will go through similar difficulties. I'll be far more likely to listen to someone who has been through the same trial I'm enduring than I will to someone quoting Bible verses and simply telling me to cheer up.

The concepts held in Romans 8:28 and James 1:2‑4 were huge foundational stones for me, but there was one more that kicked my perspective up several more notches. It was a passage that took me from being a passive observer to a proactive participant.

CORNERSTONE 3: GIVING THANKS IN EVERY SITUATION

> *Rejoice always, pray continually, give thanks in all circumstances; for this is God's will for you in Christ Jesus.* (1 Thessalonians 5:16–18)

Whoa, hold the phone!

It's one thing to believe all things work together for my good if I love God. And I'll do my best to "consider it pure joy" when I encounter problems. But to actually *give thanks* in the midst of those problems?

Sure, I see that the verse doesn't say give thanks *for* the problems, but to give thanks in the *midst* of them. Yet the words still say "in *all* circumstances." So when my puppy dog dies, I'm not only supposed to trust that God will somehow use it for my good, but I'm also actually supposed to thank Him in the middle of it?

I raced to my research books to look up the word *all*. And oddly enough, in the original language the word *all* means—hang on to your hats—"all."

And to top it off, the verse says this thanking business is "God's will for you in Christ Jesus"?

That seems crazy. What type of ivory-tower theologian would dream this up? Certainly not one who has had to face real-life issues. Maybe he should get his head out of his sanctimonious clouds and join us back here on planet Earth.

The only problem was that this theologian, the one I thought lived in an ivory tower, was the apostle Paul. And as a quick reminder, here are some of his real-life issues:

> *Five times I received from the Jews the forty lashes minus one. Three times I was beaten with rods, once I was pelted with stones, three times I was shipwrecked, I spent a night and a day in the open sea, I have been constantly on the move. I have been in danger from rivers, in danger from bandits, in danger from my fellow Jews, in danger from Gentiles; in danger in the city, in danger in the country, in danger at sea; and in danger from false believers. I have labored and toiled and have often gone without sleep; I have known hunger and thirst and have often gone without food; I have been cold and naked. Besides everything else, I face daily the pressure of my concern for all the churches.*
> (2 Corinthians 11:24–28)

And he had the audacity to consider all *that* joy and to "give thanks" for it? And then he said that giving thanks was actually God's will for him in Jesus Christ?

This is more than amazing. The guy was obviously speaking from life experience and not just rattling off religious platitudes.

Then, of course, there's that whole "all scripture is inspired by God" thing. If I was going to keep my word about always saying yes to God, then it looked like I had little choice but to give this a try as well.

And as I tested the waters and started embracing these three cornerstone principles, I grew exponentially.

I began. . .

- to view every circumstance, no matter how grim, as an opportunity to celebrate instead of a trial to endure.
- to understand that earthly thinking focuses on the circumstance, but heaven focuses on my character.
- to have more peace. As God continued to prove Himself sovereign down to the tiniest detail, I realized that He didn't need me to micromanage my life.
- to allow God to do ever greater works. Before, like a child with a splinter in his finger, I'd let Him go only so far until I screamed in pain, and in His great compassion, He would stop the procedure. Now, if I worship and adore Him even when it hurts, I free Him to go all the way and finish whatever great thing He's doing in my life.
- to experience more joy—and even anticipation. I can sincerely say, "Okay, God, this really hurts. But how cool it will be to watch the way You flip it around."

Eventually, I came to believe an important truth: "God never plays defense." No matter what the enemy throws at me, if I trust God and let Him have free rein, He will take *every* attack and use it to His glory and my blessing. It may take a while and I may never fully understand it, but if He's no liar, then I can believe that "in all things God works for the good of those who love him." In which case I can obey and "consider it pure joy. . .whenever [I] face trials." And learn to "rejoice always. . .and give thanks in all circumstances."

By living out these truths, God has proclaimed that I will sail above everything life throws at me—the pain, the confusion, and the failure. Just as wind blowing against a kite makes it fly, just as air resistance against an eagle's wings lifts it higher, if I trust God by worshipping Him In the midst of my own trials and struggles, I will be raised above every situation and I'll be empowered to soar higher into His presence and into His greatest purpose for my life.

5

THE POWER OF ADORATION

Okay, so I'd launched out on this promise to always say yes to God no matter how uninformed I felt He might be. Now I was in Rome, Italy, studying a subject I knew nothing about in a language I couldn't speak. (Please see chapter 1 for how I stumbled into this—and please read Numbers 22 to see how God uses donkeys to accomplish His will.)

I'd read the entire Bible (well, the interesting stuff anyway) and had even served as a youth worker for a local church. But for some reason, no one had ever sat me down for a serious discussion about worship. Sure, I sang the fun little songs, and I even knew the hand gestures. But I thought that's all they were—just fun, feel-good little ditties. I had no idea what would happen if I seriously engaged in them.

Then one evening I started thinking about how cool the name "Jesus Christ" sounded—how just the name "Jesus" was so soft and soothing, even loving, when you said it. I thought about how the word *Christ* sounded strong, how it had a powerful I'm-Savior-of-the-world-don't-mess-with-Me ring to it.

I was just lying there, saying His name out loud, over and over again—not chanting or reciting some mindless mantra but just marveling at the name and the person attached to it. When I got tired of doing that in English, I started saying and meditating on His name in Spanish. Then Italian. Speaking the name, yes, but more importantly, dwelling on the awesomeness of the person behind it.

Suddenly the apartment was full of light brighter than the sun, so bright I couldn't see a face, though I could just barely make out a form. I saw no name tag, heard no heavenly choir, but there was absolutely no doubt in my mind who was standing before me.

Terrifying? Let's just say I understood at that moment why the apostle John reported doing an immediate face plant when he saw Christ in His heavenly glory—and they'd been good friends during Jesus' earthly ministry (see Revelation 1:17). There was such phenomenal power and purity that the room was filled with. . .well, there was no other word for it but *glory*—so much glory that I panicked. Big-time.

No face plants for me, no sir. Instead, I chose the more cowardly route. I closed my eyes, shouting, gasping, and begging Him to leave. And His response? In contrast to that unlimited power and overwhelming glory, I heard the kindest, most understanding voice I'd ever heard.

"It's okay," He said. *"I understand. It's all right."*

And just like that, the light was gone. All trace of what had happened disappeared except for the sudden realization of what I'd done.

Are you kidding? Did you just beg the Creator of the universe to leave your apartment? Idiot! What were you thinking?

All the next day, when I wasn't calling myself out for my stupidity, I begged God to give me a second chance. "I'm young, I'm ignorant, I'm a man of unclean lips." (Hey, I tried anything.) As evening approached, I thought I'd give it another try. So once again, I kicked back and quietly meditated on His great name and His great person. And as I worshipped and adored Him, the same thing happened.

The same light, the same presence, the same unspeakable glory. What a kind and gracious God He was to give me a second chance.

And this time, after spending an entire day dwelling on what I'd done wrong and pleading for His forgiveness, this time, knowing what to expect and preparing myself for His intense presence, I again screamed and shouted and begged for Him to leave. The glory was still just too overwhelming.

And once again, I heard the kindest, gentlest voice I'd ever heard answer, *"It's okay. It's all right. I understand."* And then He was gone.

"What?" I shouted at myself. "Are you kidding me? You did it again!"

Of course I tried it a third time, but I guess Jesus pretty much figured what's the point? And believe me, over the past forty-plus years, I've tried and tried again, thousands of times—reciting my words, retracing my thoughts, looking for just the right combination to manipulate Christ into showing up again. But it has never happened. No matter what I've done, I just can't seem to make Him jump through my hoops.

Now, I'm sure this little encounter will make my anticharismatic friends nuts. The very first words out of the first pastor I told about it was, "Isn't it amazing how Satan can appear as an angel of light?"

Satan? Angel of light? I thought. *You have no idea what I saw. There's no mistaking God's glory for some fourth-rate counterfeit.*

Then there are my ultra-charismatic friends who've assured me, "If you just say this phrase or practice this gift over and over again, I'm sure there will be a manifestation."

My response to both is the same: "Sorry, but an infinite God will not be packaged into a neat, theological box, nor will He be manipulated into delivering a product, like some vending machine.

My point is, both camps have missed the point. What I took away from those encounters is this: I will never forget the power that comes from unfettered worship and adoration of God. When we intentionally and intensely worship the God of the universe with all of our hearts, all of our souls, and all of our minds, things happen. It may not be emotional, intellectual, or even predictable. And it's certainly not a way to kiss up to Him. Instead, it is joining in with the rest of the universe and responding to our Creator the way we were designed to respond.

SCRIPTURAL CONTEXT

All right, that's enough personal experience (for a while). For the record, I never trust my experiences, emotional or intellectual, if they are in conflict with the Word of God. So what does God say about worship?

A lot.

Scripture is permeated with the call for us to praise God. Here are just a few examples:

> *Enter his gates with thanksgiving and his courts with praise; give thanks to him and praise his name.* (Psalm 100:4)

> *Rejoice in the Lord always. I will say it again: Rejoice!* (Philippians 4:4)

And that's just for starters. The psalms alone include more than seventy references to praising and worshipping God. And what discussion of praise would be complete without mentioning how Jehoshaphat beat not one, not two, but three enemy armies that had ganged up to destroy Judah. His weapon of choice? Read for yourself:

> *After consulting the people, Jehoshaphat appointed men to sing to the Lord and to praise him for the splendor of his holiness as*

they went out at the head of the army, saying: "Give thanks to the Lord, for his love endures forever."

As they began to sing and praise, the Lord set ambushes against the men of Ammon and Moab and Mount Seir who were invading Judah, and they were defeated. The Ammonites and Moabites rose up against the men from Mount Seir to destroy and annihilate them. After they finished slaughtering the men from Seir, they helped to destroy one another.

When the men of Judah came to the place that overlooks the desert and looked toward the vast army, they saw only dead bodies lying on the ground; no one had escaped. So Jehoshaphat and his men went to carry off their plunder, and they found among them a great amount of equipment and clothing and also articles of value—more than they could take away. There was so much plunder that it took three days to collect it. On the fourth day they assembled in the Valley of Berakah, where they praised the Lord. This is why it is called the Valley of Berakah to this day.
(2 Chronicles 20:21–26)

While Jehoshaphat used praise for God as a weapon in a

physical battle, it is an even more devastating weapon when fighting spiritual ones. Remember that one and only exorcism I was involved with? Remember how God's Word caused the evil critters to writhe and scream?

Well, the same thing happened when I spoke words of worship. In those moments when I grew tired or started falling for the lie that the situation was hopeless, I would begin to sing a song of praise, and again the spiritual beings went ballistic, being in as much pain and agony as when I had read scripture. (Fortunately, it had nothing to do with my inability to carry a tune.)

I remember another example of the power of praise that is a bit more "normal." In our early twenties, my wife and I were backpacking through the wilderness of Israel one night (talk about young and stupid) when a pack of wild dogs came up over the ridge of a nearby hill. They were barking and carrying on, as wild packs of dogs tend to do, and they appeared on the verge of attacking us.

"They're coming!" Brenda shouted. She turned to me like I had all the answers. (She was easier to fool in those days.) "What do we do?"

"I don't know!" I yelled.

"They're going to attack!"

"I know, I know. Okay, wait a minute, I got it."

"What?"

"Sing!"

(Insert withering wife look here.)

"I'm not kidding. Sing!"

And sing we did. At the top of our lungs. And sure enough, the dogs came to a stop. They continued their barking, but they came no closer. Granted, it could be the fact that my wife's singing is almost as bad as mine, or that they thought we were rabid and didn't want to catch whatever we had. Or. . .it could be that our turning to God in an impossible situation and giving thanks had more power than we could have ever imagined.

FRINGE BENEFITS

Besides stomping demons and holding back packs of wild dogs, there are other benefits in praising God. At least two more involve peace and joy.

Before Jesus went to the cross, He made this amazing promise concerning His gift of peace: "Peace I leave with you; my peace I give you" (John 14:27).

When I worship God, I'm lifted up to the thirty-thousand-feet level, where I see worries and troubles more from His perspective. I understand He is the Master Weaver in charge of every thread that goes into weaving my tapestry.

I explored this idea much more deeply in my children's series *The Bloodstone Chronicles* (later titled *Imager Chronicles*), but it's worth repeating here. There are times I simply don't understand why I'm going through a problem, times I don't know why God has chosen to weave some dark, ugly thread into the tapestry of my life.

But those are the kinds of times when I have two choices:

1. I can kick and scream, demanding that He stop.
2. Or I can worship and adore Him, not understanding why He's doing what He's doing but somehow knowing that the dark, ugly thread will complement and bring out the beauty of all the other threads. I may not see its beauty when my nose is three inches from it, but as I worship and adore the Weaver, as I'm taken to a higher level and see the masterpiece from the Master's perspective, I'm left breathless at His artistry.

Over the years, I've so embraced this truth that I often start worshipping as soon as I slip into stress. I won't break into a rousing rendition of the "Hallelujah Chorus," but I will quietly hum some hymn or song of worship. When those closest to me hear me humming, they know something's up. My poor kids can't tell if Dad's happy or just in a really bad mood. And in the truest sense, it doesn't matter. Whether or not my mind and emotions agree, the humming aligns me more with God's perspective and subtly tells my intellect and feelings to sit down and shut up because the Master Weaver is at work.

The same holds true for joy. As the Bible teaches, "The joy of the LORD is your strength" (Nehemiah 8:10).

When I trust and believe God, my joy comes easily. On the days when I don't, I can still reach that joy, but it has to come through extended worship. And once I reach it, I can laugh at the enemy as he throws his punches, and I can chuckle (or at least smile) at the overdue bills, the lousy reviews, and the family situations going nuclear.

That doesn't mean I act irresponsibly. I still do what I can to solve the problems. But as the enemy stands outside my house taunting me, daring me to come out and fight him in my own strength, I just turn and adore God, giving Him room to flip the situation around for His glory and my benefit. As others run in panic, if I remember to worship, my faith rises to the point where I can soar above the turmoil and wait for God to pull off one of His famous eight-cushion pool table shots.

And speaking of an out-of-the-box God doing out-of-the-box things, as I'm writing this, I'm on a plane returning from delivering a series of talks about finding God's call on our lives. It's one of my favorite series, and it seemed to touch folks. But during my down-times, and a couple of weeks before, I'd been fighting discouragement about the slow progress of our media company.

I glanced at what the girl beside me was reading and saw that it was explicit vampire porn—and I mean *explicit*. I'd never read such vulgarity—and that was in just the first two sentences. She was really caught up in it, devouring page after page. As you might expect, this did not help me with my discouragement. After all, I'm trying to change the world through media, and here the media was, once again having its way by attacking another young mind.

About this time, a friend's song, titled "Holy Spirit, Come to Me," came up on my iPhone. Everybody around me, including the girl, was wearing headphones, so I leaned in as close as possible and quietly sang the song over her, replacing the word *me* with *her*. For nearly half an hour, I worshipped God and prayed over the girl. And for the first time in weeks, my own depression started lifting. I can't pretend to understand what had happened, but I do know it came about through worship.

BUT HOW?

Frankly, praising God can be tough, and at times it can seem too theoretical and abstract. I mean, it's not like we see Him every day (or in my case, every forty-plus years). But we can see His work. We may appreciate a great artist and gain insight into his work, even though we may never have a face-to-face encounter with him. The same is true with the Greatest Artist:

> *The heavens declare the glory of God; the skies*
> *proclaim the work of his hands. Day after day*

*they pour forth speech; night after night they
reveal knowledge.* (Psalm 19:1–2)
*For since the creation of the world God's
invisible qualities—his eternal power and
divine nature—have been clearly seen, being
understood from what has been made.*
(Romans 1:20)

God's artistic genius is all around us—and in us.

When I'm having a hard time worshipping, I'll often focus on a tree, or on a leaf on that tree, or an ant on that leaf. I'll sit back and quietly marvel at the mind that created these things. I'll force myself to slow down, to pause and simply enjoy childlike—and here's an important word—*wonder.*

Not long after I experienced Jesus' "guest appearance" in Rome and learned the importance of praise, I sat on the dingy back steps of my apartment, marveling at the clay-tiled roofs below me—more specifically, the color of those tiles, and even more specifically, the color orange. I know it sounds foolish, like some flashback to the hippie days, but it dawned on me that God didn't *have* to create color. It's a gift. One I should enjoy.

To this day, I try to pause and marvel. I'm a sucker when I see the rich textures that emerge in the low-angle light an hour before sunset, or the bare winter branches against a vivid blue sky, or the morning steam rising from a pond. When I choose to pause and adore the Creator of such things, I get lost in helpless wonder.

But it doesn't stop with nature. I'm astonished at the diversity of people around me as I walk through a busy airport. I think of His handiwork with each of my loved ones, how He tenderly and relentlessly shapes their souls. Then there's the artistry He loans to others—the soaring lines of architecture, the magic of electronics, and don't even get me started on museum photographs and paintings. (Seriously, if I choose to worship and adore Him in a museum, I'm only good for about a dozen paintings before I have to call it a day.)

Then there's His past work and faithfulness in my own life. . .when I think about any tough times I've endured and look back in amazement at the way good eventually triumphed over evil. Not always immediately, but always eventually.

Finally, and never to be forgotten, is the worship that bubbles up through His Word—as I study His goodness and faithfulness from centuries past:

> *Great is the Lord and most worthy of praise;*
> *his greatness no one can fathom. One gener-*
> *ation commends your works to another; they*
> *tell of your mighty acts. They speak of the*
> *glorious splendor of your majesty—and I will*
> *meditate on your wonderful works. They tell*
> *of the power of your awesome works—and I*
> *will proclaim your great deeds. They celebrate*

*your abundant goodness and joyfully sing of
your righteousness.*

*The Lord is gracious and compassionate,
slow to anger and rich in love.*

*The Lord is good to all; he has compas-
sion on all he has made. All your works praise
you, Lord; your faithful people extol you.
They tell of the glory of your kingdom and
speak of your might, so that all people may
know of your mighty acts and the glorious
splendor of your kingdom. Your kingdom is
an everlasting kingdom, and your dominion
endures through all generations.*

*The Lord is trustworthy in all he promises
and faithful in all he does. The Lord upholds all
who fall and lifts up all who are bowed down.
The eyes of all look to you, and you give them
their food at the proper time. You open your
hand and satisfy the desires of every living thing.*

*The Lord is righteous in all his ways and
faithful in all he does. The Lord is near to all
who call on him, to all who call on him in
truth. He fulfills the desires of those who fear
him; he hears their cry and saves them. The
Lord watches over all who love him, but all
the wicked he will destroy.*

My mouth will speak in praise of the

Lord. Let every creature praise his holy name
for ever and ever. (Psalm 145:3–21)

PRESSING IN

As I said earlier, worship may not always be easy—not when I'm cranky, not when the dog has just tested out his weak bladder on our new carpet, not when people cut me off on the freeway with the inappropriate but apparently obligatory hand gesture. And definitely not when I want to drop into my artistic, sackcloth-and-ashes, self-pitying melancholy.

No doubt that's why Hebrews 13:15 calls it a "sacrifice" of praise.

But doesn't worshipping God when I'm not in the mood make me a hypocrite? Or slightly schizophrenic? Or just plain living a lie?

Actually, it's the opposite. The real truth is that God is worthy of my praise even when my emotions don't feel like giving it to Him. Even when my mind thinks He doesn't deserve it.

We all know emotions and intellect can be faulty. My emotions can be manipulated by too many cups of coffee, too many computer crashes, too many minutes dealing with automated operators. My intellect can just as easily be fooled by misinformation, misinterpretation, or my own intellectual pride.

So the solution is simple for me: if I don't feel like or

think I want to praise God, my job is to tell my emotions and brain to sit down, behave themselves, and practice some truth—real truth, a truth that says God is worth every drop of praise I can squeeze out of my stubborn heart and prideful head.

THE SILENCE OF GOD

In my worst days, it can take me five, ten, even twenty minutes of forcing the praise until I really start experiencing it. Sometimes it's a bit like priming a pump or starting a reluctant lawn mower. But as I persist, the flow usually starts.

Usually.

And when it doesn't? When I don't get any sense of God's presence or His worthiness to be praised? When that silence lasts an entire day? A week? Months?

Over the years, I've discovered that those "dry" times are actually the richest times for me, my seasons of deepest blessing. No, I'm not double-talking here, and I'm not trying to sell a used god with low mileage. Seriously, when there's no intellectual appreciation, no emotional God-buzz, not even a "Sorry, God's not in, but at the sound of the tone, leave a message," those are the times that actually wind up creating my greatest growth.

That's when I double down and earnestly seek the Lord with my whole heart and my whole soul and my whole

Children
Sermon

mind. Can it by dry? Boring? Discouraging? You bet. But with no mental or emotional feel-good rewards, the only thing I have going for me is my hunger and thirst. And we know what Jesus says about that: "Blessed are those who hunger and thirst for righteousness" (Matthew 5:6).

So why is this good?

It's like a tree during a time of drought. When there's no water to reach easily near the surface, the tree sinks its roots deeper in search of moisture. That's how it is with my faith. And the dryer and longer the drought, the deeper my roots of faith dig in to find God.

Putting down roots during a drought is never pleasant. But when the violent storms of life come, when my faith is put to the test, when friends are blown over by major catastrophes, I remain standing—not only for myself, but also for them, offering shade to those who suffer from the heat and branches for those who need to rest.

When worship is dry and hard, I imagine my Personal Trainer cheering me on and encouraging me to take one last lap, even though I'm sure I don't have it in me. And the more laps I take, the stronger I grow. Nobody drifts into the Olympics. But God's great desire for us is that we become Olympians—strong, fit, and at the top of our game—for ourselves and for others.

When the dry times come, I suck it up, tell my fickle emotions and intellect to take a rest, and dive more deeply into worship. Because the longer the drought, the stronger I become.

IN SUMMARY

When a religious leader asked Jesus what the greatest commandment was, He said: " 'Love the Lord your God with all your heart and with all your soul and with all your mind.' This is the first and greatest commandment" (Matthew 22:37–38). (We'll cover the second greatest commandment, which is just as important, in a later chapter.)

Along with learning who He is, there is no faster way to fall in love with God than to worship Him. That in itself should be reason enough for us to actively pursue worship, but there's so much more. Worshipping God enables us to do the following:

- *Overcome the enemy*—both in going toe to toe with him and in dealing with the ugly situations he throws at us.
- *Experience God's peace and joy*—by allowing us to see things from the thirty-thousand-feet perspective of His absolute sovereignty.
- *See truth*—which allows us to more easily cooperate with what God is doing instead of accidentally or purposefully opposing it.

Is worship always easy? No.
Do we always feel like it? No.
Do these things matter? Not in the slightest.

And finally, we discussed the *how*. Like so many other issues of faith and obedience, the key lies in exercising our free will. It's *our* decision whether to worship, regardless of the situation or our thoughts or feelings. And it's always easier to adore God when we see the real truth of who He is, when we recall His past faithfulness, when we dwell on the wonder of His artistry, and when we bask in the greatness of who He is by reading His Word

When we film documentaries, our cameras often take a beating. All the banging and jostling throws the lenses out of alignment, making it impossible to get a clear picture. So we regularly need to take those cameras to a specialist to have them realigned. For me, that's what praise is—a realigning of my senses so they can again see the pure and accurate picture of who my Creator is and how much He loves me.

And when I see that, I can't help but fall more deeply in love.

6

REAL FREEDOM

As of this writing, our film company is developing a project that encapsulates the Gospel in thirty-second, comedic commercials for third-world-country cell phones. The idea is to present the love of Christ in a fresh, entertaining way that will encourage the audience to investigate His claims more deeply.

One of my favorite pieces is about a man trapped at the bottom of a forty-foot pit with walls so slick and slimy that it's impossible for him to climb out. Up above, folks glance down into the pit, see his plight, and just walk on by. But an intellectual professor, complete with cap and gown, takes pity on the poor man, thinks a moment, then tosses a dozen of his prized books down into the pit. Our hero is puzzled as he looks at them, but then he sets the books on the ground to stand on. They're not much help, raising him only a few feet higher.

Next comes a wealthy philanthropist, who also looks down with compassion, thinks, then uses a giant crane to lower his Mercedes into the hole. Our hero looks at the expensive car, thinks a moment, then climbs up onto the roof, but he's still impossibly far from the top of the hole.

Next comes a clergyman who dumps in robes, beads, and religious books that nearly suffocate the poor man. He fights his way through them, coughing and gagging, but is no closer to the top.

Finally, our Jesus character walks past and sees the man's condition. He climbs down into the pit, throws the fellow over his shoulder and with great effort carries him out.

Like I said, it's one of my favorite spots.

Now, if I could only believe the message behind it.

Unfortunately, I don't. Not always. Oh, I'll accept a little of Jesus' help, but more often than not I'm a firm believer of what the Bible says. . .er, make that what Ben Franklin says: "God helps those who help themselves."

And as a result, I occasionally rip off Christ of His glory.

STEALING CHRIST'S GLORY

Here's what the Word says. For the veteran Christian, it's probably old news, but as Samuel Taylor Coleridge said, "Truths are too often considered as so true they lose all the powers of truth." So bear with me and pretend this is the first time you've read this. Listen with fresh ears: "Jesus said to [Martha], 'I am the resurrection and the life. The one who believes in me will live, even though they die; and whoever lives by believing in me will never die.' " (John 11:25–26).

What is necessary for living forever?

Belief in Christ.

Here's another. Keep in mind that Jesus was referring to an event that happened when the Israelites, who'd been wandering the desert, began grumbling and complaining against Moses and God. They even accused God of bringing them out of Egypt just so they'd die. Finally, God had heard enough and sent poisonous snakes among the people, who responded by dropping dead like flies until some got the message and admitted they'd made a mistake.

God told Moses to make a bronze snake and put it on a pole. Anyone who looked up at the snake lived (Numbers 21:8–9). That's all there was to it. And that's what Jesus was talking about here:

> *"Just as Moses lifted up the snake in the wilderness, so the Son of Man must be lifted up, that everyone who believes may have eternal life in him."*
>
> *For God so loved the world that he gave his one and only Son, that whoever believes in him shall not perish but have eternal life. For God did not send his Son into the world to condemn the world, but to save the world through him. Whoever believes in him is not condemned, but whoever does not believe stands condemned already because they have not believed in the name of God's one and only Son.* (John 3:14–18)

Again, the key was simple belief. All the Israelites had to do to be saved was lift their heads and look up at the serpent. No extra work. No acts of penance. Just the simplest act of faith and they were saved. According to Jesus, the same goes for us today. We only need to be willing to look up to Him on the cross. Everything else is God's doing. It's like moving into a house completely wired for electricity. I don't have to string the cable, and I don't have to generate the power. All I have to do is have enough faith to flip the switch.

There are dozens of other passages about God doing all the heavy lifting and me just believing, but here is one more, one so deep and rich that I could think and meditate on it for days:

> But because of his great love for us, God, who is rich in mercy, made us alive with Christ even when we were dead in transgressions—it is by grace you have been saved. And God raised us up with Christ and seated us with him in the heavenly realms in Christ Jesus, in order that in the coming ages he might show the incomparable riches of his grace, expressed in his kindness to us in Christ Jesus. For it is by grace you have been saved, through faith— and this is not from yourselves, it is the gift of God—not by works, so that no one can boast. For we are God's handiwork, created in Christ Jesus to do good works, which God prepared in advance for us to do. (Ephesians 2:4–10)

Now, if I could just believe those verses. But I don't. Not all the time. God has given me this amazing free gift, but instead of enjoying it and thanking Him for it, I keep looking for ways to minimize it or, worse yet, try to *earn* it.

It's like agreeing to ride in a limo that's tooling down the freeway at 65 mph, then trying to help by getting out to push. Sure, my efforts may appear pure and grateful and noble, at least on the surface. But in reality they're motivated by pride. Worse than that, they're a slap in God's face. It's like I'm praying, "Thanks, Jesus, I really appreciate what You did on the cross, but now I'm going to earn some of God's love on my own. You don't mind if I take just a little of Your glory, do You? I mean, You couldn't have possibly done enough to get Him to love me unconditionally. But, hey, nice try. Thanks for the effort."

The problem is that this is a lose-lose mentality. Not only does Jesus lose, but so do I. The harder I work at doing, the more I wear myself out. My own accomplishments become my source of joy and fulfillment, while my own failures become a source of depression. When I win, I'm filled with pride—the same pride that subtly looks down its nose at others who aren't as impressive to God as I think I am. The same pride that judges others and, when I fail, myself. The same pride of the Pharisees, which put Jesus on the cross.

STUCK AT THE CROSS

But there's another sort of pride. A friend calls it "false humility." When he first accused me of it, I thought he meant I wasn't hiding my pride well enough, that I was faking at being humble and should be groveling and squirming more before God.

Eventually, I learned that he meant just the opposite. He meant I was stuck at the cross.

Dwelling on Christ's great sacrifice for us is a wonderful place to be. But the cross is only the beginning of the Christian walk, not the end. It's the doorway into all He wants to give us and do through us. Yet somehow I'd been taught that the more I humbled myself at the cross and hated myself for my sins, the more God would like me. Without knowing it, I was again robbing Christ of His glory. Instead of celebrating God's cleansing work and moving forward with it, I remained stuck, groveling over my unworthiness.

I'd completely ignored the book of Romans, which says (or implies) nearly fifty times that my "old man" is dead. Actually, I didn't ignore it—I just didn't believe it. I felt even guiltier each time I failed and sinned, begging God to kill me all over again because apparently He had failed the first time. But the truth was, if I *really* believed the power of His work on the cross, if I *really* believed His Word, then my old man *really* was dead.

But I couldn't believe it. Instead, I kept visiting the

cemetery, feeling guilty over a corpse that in God's eyes was already dead. Worst yet, I kept digging it up and trying to rehabilitate it when, according to God, Christ's work had made me a totally new creature, even though I didn't always behave like one.

This was a tough truth to wrap my head around. But God said it, so I either had to either believe it or call Him a liar. When I chose to believe it, I was able to leave the cross behind. I was able to cross over and enter the promised land and actually be the new creation Christ had made me. Instead of trying to rehabilitate the dead me that I had been dwelling on and He completely ignored, I started focusing on the new me that God saw. He has no interest in the old and dead me that died with Jesus on the cross. Instead, His focus is now on the new me who is in Christ. Paul clarified that point when he wrote, "If Christ is in you, then even though your body is subject to death because of sin, the Spirit gives life because of righteousness" (Romans 8:10).

Whether my mind accepted it, whether my emotions felt like it, the new me was the only me that existed because it was the only me God chose to acknowledge. Or, as my friend is so fond of saying: "God no longer sees what is wrong with you; He only sees what is missing."

Grasping this truth was a huge brain shift for me. I used to figure that God forgave me, but grudgingly. Now I began seeing myself as totally new and truly free of the old corpse, *even when my habits and failures said otherwise.* That's freedom, and not just from condemnation when I meet God in heaven, but here and now, even when I fail.

Besides inventing the cross, the Romans created another hideous form of execution. They would tie a dead and rotting corpse to a criminal's back. Wherever the man went, the decaying flesh (swarming with maggots and with a putrid stench) went, until the prisoner eventually died from disease and exhaustion.

That had been me—a Christian who thought I had to carry around my old man—until I finally embraced the truth that Christ had cut me lose and I was free.

Do I still sin? Yes. Old habits die hard. But I don't dwell on them. I don't let the devil tell me I'm a loser. I no longer beat myself up and take a time-out and stand in the corner, feeling like I have to pay for something Jesus already paid for. Instead, I repent as quickly as possible and run back into my Father's arms. The faster I do it, the more it proves Christ's victory. Because the longer I wait, thinking God is mad at me, the more I steal the glory from Christ.

God doesn't get mad at me. Not even on my worst days. Not even in my worst sins. He already got mad at Jesus. Now, like the dad in the story of the prodigal son, He waits with outstretched arms for me to "come to my senses" and return to His love, where we can focus on the new nature He's created and is so excited for me to grow into.

The more I understand this, the more I see myself as God sees me through Christ's sacrifice, the more I can grasp verses like this: "The LORD your God is with you, the Mighty Warrior who saves. He will take great delight in you; in his love he will no longer rebuke you, but will rejoice over you with singing" (Zephaniah 3:17).

Can you imagine God actually singing over you? Even when you've sinned? (I'll wait for you to go back and make sure that's not a typo.) Well, He does. He does that because He now sees you in Christ. He sees you as He chooses to see you, through His Son's blood. And what God chooses to see is the only truth there is.

Talk about the Gospel! Talk about Good News!

But wait, it gets better. . . .

FRIENDS WITH GOD

Not only is my old corpse dead, not only is all my bad be-behavior forgiven, but Christ's sacrifice on the cross was so great that it actually made me His friend:

> "Greater love has no one than this: to lay down one's life for one's friends. You are my friends if you do what I command. I no longer call you servants, because a servant does not know his master's business. Instead, I have called you friends, for everything that I learned from my Father I have made known to you." (John 15:13–15)

And this friendship didn't stop with His apostles. Just a little bit later, when He prayed over the boys, He also included us:

> "My prayer is not for them alone. I pray also for those who will believe in me through their message, that all of them may be one, Father, just as you are in me and I am in you. May they also be in us so that the world may believe that you have sent me. I have given them the glory that you gave me, that they may be one as we are one—I in them and you in me." (John 17:20–23)

AND BETTER STILL. . .

God wants to be *more* intimate with us than a friend. As I've said, at least eighteen times in the Bible, God refers to us, in one form or another, as His bride: "As a bridegroom rejoices over his bride, so will your God rejoice over you" (Isaiah 62:5).

When I speak publically, I often use an illustration a friend has agreed to let me borrow. I bring two men from the audience up on stage. One represents the Father, the other represents Christ. I have them stand close, facing one another as I talk about the phenomenal love between God the Father and God the Son. That's a love that existed before the creation of the world, a love so perfect, so intense and pure that their Spirit is locked together in union so that somehow they are literally one in the same.

Then I say, "The Father tells His Son to go to earth and find a bride."

The man playing Christ (whom I've checked beforehand to see that he is married) goes out into the audience and chooses his wife. She takes his hand, and he brings her up on stage.

"Now," I say, "as a member of your family, where are you going to put her?"

Not expecting this question, he hesitates, but only for a moment, before choosing to place her between the Father and himself.

Not once in all the times I've used this illustration has the husband left his bride on the outside. He has *always* placed her in between the Father and himself. And with all of Jesus' promises that we are in Him just as He is in the Father and the Father is in Him, there is little doubt that He, too, has placed us smack dab in the middle of the family love-fest.

And what did the woman playing the bride do to receive this highly favored position? She simply took her husband's hand when he reached out to her, which is all we have to do with Christ.

Most theologians believe the Song of Songs has been

kept in the sacred writings as a metaphor of the great love between Jesus Christ and His bride. And no talk of the church being Christ's adored bride would be complete without verses like these:

> *You are altogether beautiful, my darling; there is no flaw in you.* (Song of Songs 4:7)

> *You have stolen my heart, my sister, my bride; you have stolen my heart with one glance of your eyes, with one jewel of your necklace. How delightful is your love, my sister, my bride! How much more pleasing is your love than wine, and the fragrance of your perfume than any spice! Your lips drop sweetness as the honeycomb, my bride; milk and honey are under your tongue. The fragrance of our garments is like the fragrance of Lebanon.* (Song of Songs 4:9–11)

And keep in mind that the author of the book was living in a desert region:

> *You are a garden locked up, my sister, my bride; you are a spring enclosed, a sealed fountain. . . . You are a garden fountain, a well of flowing water.* (Song of Songs 4:12, 15)

This is the passion, the intense love God has for us, His beloved bride.

As I mentioned in an earlier chapter, the next time you go to a wedding, make a big deal about the bride as she comes down the aisle. But if you can, steal a glance back at the groom and check out the look of love on his face. And remember that's exactly what Jesus Christ feels for you every moment of your life. He has the same love, the same passion a groom has for his bride on their wedding day.

OUR TRUE POSITION

Not only are we the beloved bride that Jesus loved more than His own life, but we are also His chosen co-rulers of the universe. Better read that over again, too. Better yet, try reading these passages:

> *The Spirit himself testifies with our spirit that we are God's children. Now if we are children, then we are heirs—heirs of God and co-heirs with Christ.* (Romans 8:16–17)

And just to keep things interesting, there's this:

> *Do you not know that we will judge angels?*
> (1 Corinthians 6:3)

God raised us up with Christ and seated us
with him in the heavenly realms in Christ
Jesus. (Ephesians 2:6)

"To the one who is victorious, I will give the
right to sit with me on my throne, just as I
was victorious and sat down with my Father
on his throne." (Revelation 3:21)

DEFEATING THE GREAT ACCUSER

When those times of doubting how highly honored you are
come, when you think you're such a piece of work that even
Christ's great love and sacrifice isn't enough, don't feel bad.
No need to feel guilty about feeling guilty. Just keep in mind
that you may be having some supernatural help (from the
wrong side) with those *I-hate-me* thoughts.

Another biblical name for Satan is the "accuser of our
brothers and sisters" (Revelation 12:10), and frankly, he's a
pro at it. Scripture says he accused us day and night before
God hurled him down to the earth. Now, apparently, the
only ones who believe him or take his accusations seriously
are us. The accuser accuses us to us, and we're the only ones
falling for his lie.

So what's the remedy?

Once again, it comes down to faith. Do we take Satan's

word or God's word? Do we trust our emotions or God's promises? Do we keep our eyes fixed on Jesus and walk on water, or do we take our eyes off Him, look down at ourselves, and sink?

BE FREE

The next time you feel like talking trash about God's bride (that's you) and dare to call it humility, get over yourself and give Jesus the credit He deserves. He died an indescribable death, taking on *all* your failures. It's no longer about you or what you've done (either good or bad). It's now about Jesus and what He's done. Stop stealing His glory. Stop trying to be more demanding of yourself than God.

When Jesus visited His hometown synagogue, He made the official announcement of His mission. This is what happened:

> *The scroll of the prophet Isaiah was handed to him. Unrolling it, he found the place where it is written: "The Spirit of the Lord is on me, because he has anointed me to proclaim good news to the poor. He has sent me to proclaim freedom for the prisoners and recovery of sight for the blind, to set the oppressed free, to proclaim the year of the Lord's favor." Then he*

*rolled up the scroll, gave it back to the atten-
dant and sat down. The eyes of everyone in
the synagogue were fastened on him. He began
by saying to them, "Today this scripture is
fulfilled in your hearing."* (Luke 4:17–21)

The cross set me free—free of my old man, free of guilt over every failure, free to see myself as the Father sees me. Because of Jesus' great sacrifice, I am no longer a groveling slave. I am now free to be:

- God's child
- God's friend
- God's bride

But so many of us—in our pious, false humility—call God a liar and act like His Word isn't true. We won't believe Him, so we stay stuck on the wrong side of the cross. We've twisted the very act that was intended to free us and made it into a wall to block us. Instead of entering into God's promises through the door of the cross, we drop to our knees and refuse to step through. And then we disguise it by calling it humility and gratitude.

Many liken receiving Christ as Savior to Israel crossing the Jordan and entering the promised land. After years of slavery and wandering in the desert, they finally crossed over and took what God had promised them. The problem was they only took 10 percent of what had been promised and refused to claim the other 90 percent.

The same was true of myself and remains true of many Christians today. We've crossed the Jordan, received our cleansing, and entered what God promised to be a new and powerful life. But once we got on the other side, our faith faltered and we failed to believe the greatness of His gift. We chose to take only a small percentage of what God Himself wanted to give us. Instead of grabbing hold and rejoicing in all He has given us, instead of using our new position to change the world, we cowered, we grew fearful, and then we dared call it humility.

What a lie!

What a waste of God's death!

Don't settle for the lie. Live your freedom. Celebrate it. Rejoice in it. When you stumble, don't steal Christ's glory by taking a time out. Instead, use it as an opportunity to immediately run into God's arms and praise His Son even more greatly. Christ loved you more than His own life. Give Him that honor and glory. Give Him that love.

If you've made a commitment to Christ, God has absolutely nothing against you. He no longer sees what's wrong, only what's missing—and He's excited to give you what you lack.

What would you do differently today if you truly believed that God loves you—I mean *really* loves you? One of my favorite prayers, which I seldom pray out loud but fervently pray to the Father in secret, is this: *Lord, help me love You and take as much joy in You as you love and take joy in me.*

7

TRUTH AND GRACE

Does all this talk about God adoring us and taking great joy over us, even when we fail, provide a free pass to sin?

No. God is no fool. We can't con or manipulate Him.

But if I've given my life to Christ, am honest about my faults, and am aiming for holiness, He will *never* keep track of my times of failure. And He'll always be there to help me to my feet, give me a hug, and whisper into my ear, "Okay, son, what say we give that another try."

Jesus is on my side even when I fail. He understands my temptations and wants to forgive me. So when I fall, I try not to run and hide from Him. (Where do you hide from God anyway?) Instead, I fall toward His open arms so He can forgive me and quickly get back to His plan of making me, "mature and complete, not lacking anything" (James 1:4).

That's some love. That's some God

So as you read this chapter, *do not* feel condemned. For, as Paul says, "Therefore, there is now no condemnation for those who are in Christ Jesus" (Romans 8:1).

Feel challenged, feel exhorted, feel inspired to do better, but never listen to your accuser and allow him to make you feel like a loser.

THE JOY OF OBEDIENCE

"Everything is permissible"—but not everything is beneficial. "Everything is permissible"—but not everything is constructive. (1 Corinthians 10:23)

Every year Seattle has a celebration called Seafair. When I was a little guy, I used to love going to the Seafair Parade. There were marching bands, dignitaries waving from cars, and vendors selling balloons. But the thing I loved most was the Seafair pirates float. It would roll down the street, and the Seafair pirates would reach into huge barrels, scoop up handfuls of candy, and throw it out to the crowds lining the parade route. Then the kids would run out, screaming and fighting, pushing and shoving, to get a piece of candy as the parents laughed and clapped and shouted encouragement.

This was called "entertainment."

One time when I was four or five, we arrived along the parade route early, finding the perfect spot to sit on the curb. From there I would be able to race ahead of the other kids and get a piece of candy, maybe two. But as the float approached and I prepared to make my move, my mom bent down to me and said, "Billy, I don't want you going out there."

What? I couldn't believe my ears. I had the perfect seat. I was primed and ready. And now I was just supposed to sit there and watch everyone else but me run out to get their prize? Talk about unfair! It made no sense (and it still doesn't to this day), but I obeyed. I sat there brokenhearted, tears streaming down my face as the pirates threw candy and all my friends screamed and fought and laughed and pushed for their piece.

I'll never forget the pain and disappointment.

But there's something else I'll never forget: As the float approached, it slowed to a stop directly in front of us. Then the strangest thing happened. Through my tears, I saw the head pirate reach into the barrel and pull out a giant handful of candy. He stepped down from the float and, in front of everybody, walked directly to me, bent over, and dumped the entire handful into my lap. He whispered something into my ear (which I was too stunned to hear, much less remember) then climbed back onto the float, which continued down the street.

Even as I write this, I feel my throat tightening. This incident changed my life. And at the tender age of four or five, I learned the advantage of obedience, even when it didn't make sense. I learned that if I focus on doing God's will, everything else will fall into place: "But seek first his kingdom and his righteousness, and all these things will be given to you as well" (Matthew 6:33).

Could I have disobeyed? You bet. I was in the perfect spot to get out there and get several pieces of candy. But that wouldn't have been nearly as good as getting a lapful. More importantly, it wouldn't have been as good as the lesson I learned about obedience.

IS OBEDIENCE NECESSARY?

Scripture says, "If you declare with your mouth, 'Jesus is Lord,' and believe in your heart that God raised him from the dead, you will be saved" (Romans 10:9), but it also says the following:

> *What shall we say, then? Shall we go on sinning so that grace may increase? By no means! We are those who have died to sin; how can we live in it any longer? Or don't you know that all of us who were baptized into Christ Jesus were baptized into his death? We were therefore buried with him through baptism into death in order that, just as Christ was raised from the dead through the glory of the Father, we too may live a new life.* (Romans 6:1–4)

> *But among you there must not be even a hint of sexual immorality, or of any kind of impurity, or of greed, because these are improper for God's holy people.* (Ephesians 5:3)

> *For God did not call us to be impure, but to live a holy life.* (1 Thessalonians 4:7)

> *Therefore, with minds that are alert and fully*
> *sober, set your hope on the grace to be brought*
> *to you when Jesus Christ is revealed at his*
> *coming. As obedient children, do not conform*
> *to the evil desires you had when you lived in*
> *ignorance. But just as he who called you is*
> *holy, so be holy in all you do; for it is written:*
> *"Be holy, because I am holy." Since you call*
> *on a Father who judges each person's work*
> *impartially, live out your time as foreigners*
> *here in reverent fear.* (1 Peter 1:13–17)

The Bible has plenty to say about how God calls His people to lives of obedience. But asking if obedience is necessary for salvation is asking the wrong question. My new life is a love relationship with God, so asking if I have to obey Him is like asking if I have to be nice to my wife. If I have to ask such a question, then there's something wrong with the relationship.

God wants me to be holy and to obey Him (mostly, I believe, because I'm the one who benefits). But—and this is a hugely important "but"—obedience is *not* my goal. My goal is my relationship with Jesus Christ—to go deeper, to fall more in love, to become so intimate that we literally become one. Holiness and righteousness are merely the thermometers telling me how hot that love is. And the deeper I abide in Christ, the higher that temperature rises.

I would die for my wife and kids. Not because it's in some marriage contract, and not because I joined some program teaching me how to die for my family. I would give my life for them because my love for them is so intense that I can't help myself.

That's what holiness is: doing the right thing at any cost because of love.

I don't act in righteousness to earn God's love. I act in righteousness *because* of His love. It's the difference between night and day.

Oh, and one other thing. . .

I'M INCAPABLE OF RIGHTEOUSNESS ON MY OWN

> *So I find this law at work: Although I want to do good, evil is right there with me. For in my inner being I delight in God's law; but I see another law at work in me, waging war against the law of my mind and making me a prisoner of the law of sin at work within me. What a wretched man I am! Who will rescue me from this body that is subject to death? Thanks be to God, who delivers me through Jesus Christ our Lord!* (Romans 7:21–25)

Not only are we delivered from the penalty of sin through

Jesus Christ, but He actually gives us the power *not* to sin.

If I'm struggling with a specific sin, I don't focus on not committing that sin. That would be like being a junk food addict who is on a diet staring at a side of piping-hot french fries and saying, "I will not eat those! I will not eat those! I will not eat those!" That self-control may last for a day or a week, but if that addict constantly sees the fries, dreams about them, and smells them, his thinking will eventually go like this: *Well, it won't hurt to try just one. All right, maybe two.* And there goes the diet.

But if that addict can replace those fries with something that smells and tastes better and that just happens to make him feel better, then their hold on him disappears. The same is true with sin. Instead of dwelling on my sin and telling myself I will not do it, I dwell on something a thousand times better—my love for Jesus Christ and His love for me.

But it's more than just some emotional mind game. Something supernatural also happens. Jesus put it best when He said:

> "I am the true vine, and my Father is the gardener. He cuts off every branch in me that bears no fruit, while every branch that does bear fruit he prunes so that it will be even more fruitful. You are already clean because of the word I have spoken to you. Remain in me, as I also remain in you. No branch can bear

fruit by itself; it must remain in the vine.
Neither can you bear fruit unless you remain
in me. I am the vine; you are the branches.
If you remain in me and I in you, you will
bear much fruit; apart from me you can do
nothing." (John 15:1–5)

In my orchard, I never hear my fruit trees screaming and groaning as they struggle to bear fruit. Growing fruit just comes to them naturally. As long as the branches are connected to the trunk, they bear fruit.

The same is true with Jesus and me. If I don't like the fruit in my life, I don't try to fix the fruit. I look at my connection to the vine and the trunk. That's where the power comes from. When there's sin in my life, I don't examine it, looking for ways to do better. I examine my relationship with Jesus and find ways to deepen it. And the deeper and stronger that connection grows, the more His power flows through me, and the more victory I have over sin.

Once again, we see the difference between being a follower of Jesus and simply being religious. Forget the list of rules. There are no lists in a love relationship. There's only love, and everything else grows naturally out of that love.

JUDGING OTHERS

Once I grasped this concept and really made it my own, I discovered another benefit: I stopped judging others.

This was huge for a good, rule-following, squeaky-clean Christian boy. If I worked so hard to cross every *t* and dot every *i* in my life (so God wouldn't hate me), then I could only imagine how much He hated those who weren't even trying.

Oh sure, I covered up my judgmental attitude with patronizing smiles, but inside I gave the slacker no slack. Christian or not, it made no difference. I looked at everybody through my own lens of success or failure instead of through Christ's lens of love and sacrifice.

It's true that a time of judgment will come. But not now. Now is the time Christ's arms are wide open to receive anybody and everybody, no matter how vile. I'm not called to judge any person. I'm not even called to clean him up and make him presentable. I'm called to love him and introduce him to the One who will do the cleaning and presenting.

I'll never forget this great quote by a pastor: "If you take the time to wash a person's feet, you will see why they limp." Even the world's worst offender is not my enemy. Nor God's. He is merely a prisoner of war of a far greater enemy, one who wants to kill and destroy him. And it is my joy to love him and point him to the One who can set him free.

DISCIPLINE, NOT PUNISHMENT

Does Christ's sacrifice on the cross mean that God never punishes people for their sin? Well, ask a married couple named Ananias and Sapphira:

> *Now a man named Ananias, together with his wife Sapphira, also sold a piece of property. With his wife's full knowledge he kept back part of the money for himself, but brought the rest and put it at the apostles' feet.*
>
> *Then Peter said, "Ananias, how is it that Satan has so filled your heart that you have lied to the Holy Spirit and have kept for yourself some of the money you received for the land? Didn't it belong to you before it was sold? And after it was sold, wasn't the money at your disposal? What made you think of doing such a thing? You have not lied just to human beings but to God."*
>
> *When Ananias heard this, he fell down and died. And great fear seized all who heard what had happened. Then some young men came forward, wrapped up his body, and carried him out and buried him.*
>
> *About three hours later his wife came in, not knowing what had happened. Peter asked*

> *her, "Tell me, is this the price you and Ananias*
> *got for the land?"*
>
> *"Yes," she said, "that is the price."*
>
> *Peter said to her, "How could you conspire*
> *to test the Spirit of the Lord? Listen! The feet*
> *of the men who buried your husband are at*
> *the door, and they will carry you out also."*
>
> *At that moment she fell down at his feet*
> *and died. Then the young men came in and,*
> *finding her dead, carried her out and buried*
> *her beside her husband.* (Acts 5:1–10)

Serious stuff. But remember, this couple knew the truth but instead of coming clean and admitting their failure, as God requires, they tried to cover it up. Worse yet, they tried lying to Him. It would have been an entirely different outcome if they had admitted their deceit and asked for forgiveness.

Later, when the apostle John was writing the book of Revelation, he also received some serious words warning six churches to get their acts together. If they didn't, there would be major consequences. It's hard knowing if they obeyed, but it's interesting to note that none of those churches exist today.

Still, I believe these are the exceptions, extreme measures necessary for extreme sin. The New Testament constantly refers to God as a loving Father who agreed to let

His Son die on the cross for our failures. Granted, He has not changed since He dealt out the wrath and punishment in the Old Testament, but He has drawn up an entirely new contract (covenant) with us. In this new contract, someone still has to pay for all our sins and unrighteousness. But this time that someone is God Himself.

Nevertheless, this doesn't stop Him from being a loving father who disciplines His children. After all, that's for our good. But it's discipline, not punishment. That's what a loving parent does. As the writer of the epistle to the Hebrews says:

> *And have you completely forgotten this word of encouragement that addresses you as a father addresses his son? It says, "My son, do not make light of the Lord's discipline, and do not lose heart when he rebukes you, because the Lord disciplines the one he loves, and he chastens everyone he accepts as his son."*
>
> *Endure hardship as discipline; God is treating you as his children. For what children are not disciplined by their father? If you are not disciplined—and everyone undergoes discipline—then you are not legitimate, not true sons and daughters at all. Moreover, we have all had human fathers who disciplined us and we respected them for it. How much*

> *more should we submit to the Father of spirits*
> *and live! They disciplined us for a little while*
> *as they thought best; but God disciplines us*
> *for our good, in order that we may share in*
> *his holiness. No discipline seems pleasant at*
> *the time, but painful. Later on, however, it*
> *produces a harvest of righteousness and peace*
> *for those who have been trained by it.*
> (Hebrews 12:5–11)

One time my cameraman and I were flying home from a shoot in Bolivia. We'd been in the jungles, traveled mountain roads for weeks, and we were dead tired. We found a row on the plane with three open seats and sat with the vacant seat between us so we could spread out and relax. But the plane was getting more crowded by the second. When people approached and asked us if the empty seat was taken, we pretended like we didn't understand them. If they spoke Spanish, we spoke English. If they spoke English, we spoke French.

Bottom line, we were being jerks.

But it worked. The entire plane filled up except for the one and only vacant seat between us. Ah, sweet victory! We'd gotten our way. But even as the door shut, part of me felt bad. It wasn't so much guilt as it was disappointment. If God really loved us, why did He let His two kids get off with such behavior? As the props revved up and the plane started forward, I began thinking of the above passage in Hebrews.

But we had only taxied a dozen feet before the props died down and the plane coasted to a stop. That's when I looked out the window and saw—I kid you not—a woman weighing at least 250 pounds waddling out of the terminal. In one hand was a giant grocery bag and in the other. . .a crying baby. She climbed on board, and of course, there was only one place left to sit.

Though we were incredibly cramped during the hours of flight, I giggled to myself and felt pretty good. God had not let me down. I was still His beloved son.

ALL THIS TO SAY. . .

God is absolute love.

He is also absolute holiness.

That's why we needed a new contract—a contract calling for Jesus to die on the cross for all our failures so God could pour out His extravagant love on us even when we fail miserably.

But that doesn't negate the importance and benefits of obedience.

Still, keep in mind that obedience is not the endgame. It is merely an indicator of the depth of our love. Our first call is to love God with all of our heart, soul, mind, and strength. If that is our pursuit, everything else will fall into place. Or, as Jesus Himself says: "If you remain in me and I in you, you will bear much fruit; apart from me you can do nothing" (John 15:5).

God has agreed to do all the heavy lifting. All we have to do is be honest with Him, ask for His help, and allow Him to lavish His unending love on us. All we have to do is allow ourselves to be part of the greatest love story in the history of the universe.

8

↔

AND NOW FOR SOME FRUIT

By putting so much emphasis on abiding in Christ's love—and not as much on serving Him—it might become easy to take things out of context. Some of the New Testament era Christians apparently did just that. That's probably why James, the leader of the church in Jerusalem at the time, wrote the following:

> *What good is it, my brothers and sisters, if someone claims to have faith but has no deeds? Can such faith save them? Suppose a brother or a sister is without clothes and daily food. If one of you says to them, "Go in peace; keep warm and well fed," but does nothing about their physical needs, what good is it? In the same way, faith by itself, if it is not accompanied by action, is dead.*
>
> *But someone will say, "You have faith; I have deeds." Show me your faith without deeds, and I will show you my faith by my deeds. You believe that there is one God. Good! Even the demons believe that—and shudder.* (James 2:14–19)

Apparently, some folks thought that if having faith in Jesus Christ and loving Him was all that mattered, then all they would do was have faith in Jesus Christ and love Him. They seemed to believe that now that they were saved, they could just kick back and lounge around until they died and cruised into heaven.

Of course that begs the question, once we're saved, why even waste time here—why not just go directly to heaven?

The obvious answer is that there's still plenty to do down here on earth. With Christ's physical presence gone, you and I are now His hands and arms, His feet and legs. We are Christ's body here on earth. And as Christ's body, we are called to love, embrace, and help others just as He did.

Bono, the singer for the rock group U2, points out that the only time Jesus made a clear distinction between those going to heaven and those going to hell was when He spoke this parable:

> "When the Son of Man comes in his glory, and all the angels with him, he will sit on his glorious throne. All the nations will be gathered before him, and he will separate the people one from another as a shepherd separates the sheep from the goats. He will put the sheep on his right and the goats on his left.
>
> "Then the King will say to those on his right, 'Come, you who are blessed by my Father; take your inheritance, the kingdom prepared for you since the creation of the world. For I was hungry and you gave me something to eat, I was thirsty and you gave

me something to drink, I was a stranger and you invited me in, I needed clothes and you clothed me, I was sick and you looked after me, I was in prison and you came to visit me.'

"Then the righteous will answer him, 'Lord, when did we see you hungry and feed you, or thirsty and give you something to drink? When did we see you a stranger and invite you in, or needing clothes and clothe you? When did we see you sick or in prison and go to visit you?'

"The King will reply, 'Truly I tell you, whatever you did for one of the least of these brothers and sisters of mine, you did for me.'

"Then he will say to those on his left, 'Depart from me, you who are cursed, into the eternal fire prepared for the devil and his angels. For I was hungry and you gave me nothing to eat, I was thirsty and you gave me nothing to drink, I was a stranger and you did not invite me in, I needed clothes and you did not clothe me, I was sick and in prison and you did not look after me.'

"They also will answer, 'Lord, when did we see you hungry or thirsty or a stranger or needing clothes or sick or in prison, and did not help you?'

> *"He will reply, 'Truly I tell you, whatever*
> *you did not do for one of the least of these, you*
> *did not do for me.'*
> *"Then they will go away to eternal pun-*
> *ishment, but the righteous to eternal life."*
> (Matthew 25:31–46)

This is a serious word, and much needed, particularly in today's world, where there are such staggering needs—needs so overwhelming that it's easy to overload and just go numb (and then feel guilty for going numb). But there's a simple solution. It's the answer to the old children's riddle, "How do you eat an elephant?" The answer? "One bite at a time."

It's impossible for one person to do everything. And here, once again, I rely on God to call the shots. I listen for that still, small voice to say, "This is the one, so pay attention." Or I'll trust Him to put situations before me. Sometimes it's the great and grand programs that everyone is rallying behind, but just as often, it's the little, seemingly inconsequential, needs I see around me—the employee sitting by himself at the lunch table, the relative trying to make ends meet on a shrinking Social Security check, the homeless person who needs to be treated with the same honor and respect God has for him.

Not long ago, I played a homeless man in a movie. We were filming on Hollywood Boulevard at night, and the camera crew was on the other side of the wide, four-lane street.

No actors or crew were around me, so passersby figured I was the real deal. In a theater just down the street, a stage production let out, and the wealthy patrons—hundreds of them—swarmed out and toward their cars. And not a one, not a single person, even bothered to look at me. I was nonhuman, totally invisible to everybody—except for one person.

A black man, dressed only a little better than I was that night, waited at a bus stop. Spotting me, he walked over and said, "Where do I put it, man?"

I looked up. "Pardon me?"

"You got no can, no box." He opened his palm, showing a handful of coins. "Where do I put it?"

Amazing. Here we were, surrounded by wealthy people who acted like I didn't exist, and a black man, nearly my age (meaning he probably experienced the racial hatred and bigotry that came with that era), asked how to give this poor white man some money.

That's serving, God-style. Or as Jesus said, "Whatever you did for one of the least of these brothers of mine, you did for me."

Another verse I keep in mind when choosing whom to serve also comes from James' practical, no-nonsense thinking: "Religion that God our Father accepts as pure and faultless is this: to look after orphans and widows in their distress and to keep oneself from being polluted by the world" (James 1:27).

Besides the call to holiness, which we discussed in the

last chapter, James pointed to helping the weakest and most defenseless of his time. So I ask myself, *In my own world, who is the weakest? Who is the most defenseless? Is it the unborn child? Is it the one out of eight people in the world going to bed hungry? The orphaned refugees living in a country devastated by war?*

The possibilities are nearly endless, and they call us to listen carefully and look to God's will.

But with such overwhelming needs around us, it's easy to get the cart before the horse—to run ahead and put serving in front of abiding. And once we start down that slope, we're pulled right back into a works mentality where

- we measure our standing with God by our service to Him.
- we judge others, and ourselves, by accomplishments (and failures).
- we see people and circumstances as a means to an end instead of the primary purpose.

Before you know it, we're back on that religious hamster wheel, running to please God, running to accomplish His projects.

A CONTRADICTION?

What I've written above brings us to an important question: do the ideas of serving and abiding contradict one another? Absolutely not! It's a paradox. It's God holding two seemingly opposing viewpoints at the same time.

Those who like to keep God in a box hate paradoxes. I love them. Paradoxes simply prove there is a bigger answer than the question I'm asking. God is so infinite that when I ask if His answer is A or B, He'll often say something like, "Oranges."

And He'll be right!

Faith without works is as useless as works without faith. You cannot have one without the other. But it is not a question of which came first—like the old chicken-or-egg riddle. Faith and relationship must always proceed service until the two eventually comingle and become gloriously intertwined.

In my novel *Child's Play*, a comedy that takes place in a mental ward in the future where faith has been outlawed, one of the patients opens a fortune cookie that reads: "You are my favorite child. God." For days the residents dwell on this concept, mulling it over and over. The players are Bernie, our narrator (who has wonderful conversations with people's tattoos and electrical appliances); Ralphy, a superhero complete with shower cap, goggles, and bath towel cape; Nelson, a savant with a photographic memory; Winona, who is convinced she's an alien from another planet; and

Joey, who is certain the earth is flat.

When faced with a similar question of relationship versus religion, the following is the answer that Max, their leader, comes up with:

> *Again, Max shook his head. He thought a moment, then said, "Bernie, will you hand me that tablet and pen on my desk?"*
>
> *I scooped them up and passed them to him. He thought another moment, then he drew a big circle a little to the left side of the page. Inside and at the top left of it, he wrote the word HEART.*

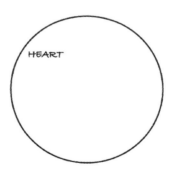

> *"It's as if this is my heart," he said. "All of my emotions, all my feelings."*
>
> *I leaned in for a better look.*
>
> *He continued, "But they're not always right, are they? We can't always trust our emotions."*

"Affirmative," Winona said. "Feelings interfere with the intellectual process. It is the strength of the mind that marks a superiorly evolved race."

"Really?" he said. "Is that really true?"

Before she answered, he drew another circle on the right half of the page. Near the top, he wrote the word MIND. But like the HEART circle, it was too big to stay on its side of the paper, so the two circles overlapped in the middle.

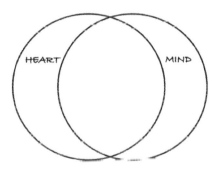

"Is the mind always right?" he asked. "Aren't we constantly replacing outdated facts with newer and more accurate ones?"

"He's got a point," Joey said.

"Like the earth may actually be round?" she shot back.

Joey shook his head, subtly taking hold of his chair. "Unsubstantiated rumors."

"We have pictures."

"Photoshop."

Max ignored them and pointed to the smaller space where the two circles overlapped. "And this section here, what would you call it?"

We stared at the picture real hard, but no one had an answer.

"Isn't this who we really are?" Max said. "We're not simply heart, and we're not simply mind, but aren't we a combination of both?"

"In my country, one would call such a thing the soul," Ralphy said. "It is the soul that makes up the true man."

Max nodded and wrote out the word SOUL in the smaller space.

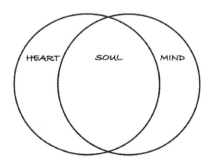

Nelson began bobbing. " 'Love the Lord your God with all your HEART and with all your SOUL and with all your MIND.' "

No one said anything as we all just stared at the paper.

"But I think there's one more part," Max said. "I think we're leaving something out. It's what Nelson, Bernie, and I discussed earlier this morning." He looked at me like I had the answer.

I smiled but was clueless.

He looked down and began drawing a tiny little circle inside the SOUL space, and then he colored it in.

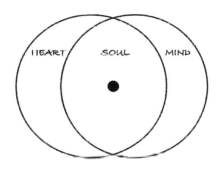

"What is that?" Joey said.

"I think. . . Now remember this is all new to me. But I think that part. . . I think it is the Spirit."

"The what?"

"The Spirit of God."

"Sure is puny," Joey said, "compared to the other parts, I mean."

"At first, yes. But, like anything else, if I

feed it, it grows."

"What do you mean," Winona said. "How do you feed it?"

"It's like we said earlier, by remaining in God's presence. By feeding on Him."

Nelson bobbed. " 'The one who feeds on Me will live because of Me.' "

We were all too surprised to speak.

"And there's more." Max started getting even more excited. "As I feed on Him, as His Spirit grows inside of me, it starts influencing me." He drew arrows shooting out from the little circle. Then he made a bigger circle around them.

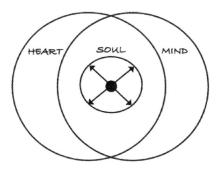

"It starts directing my heart and my mind—helping me feel things the way He feels them, and to think about things the way He thinks about them." He drew the arrows even bigger, out to the very edge.

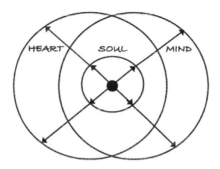

Nelson gave another quote, "'You, however, are controlled not by the sinful nature but by the Spirit, if the Spirit of God lives in you.'" He paused, then added, "'For it is God who works in you to will and to act according to His good purpose.'"

Max nodded. "God. . .not me. God. I don't have to do all those good things that make people good or moral or religious. And I don't have to avoid all the bad things that make people bad."

"God does it for you," Joey said.

"Right. Goodness is still my goal. It's just how I get there. Instead of trying to do it on my own, where I'm always failing and feeling guilty, I let God do it. And the best thing is, it happens naturally. . .as naturally as a tree growing fruit."

Again Nelson quoted, "'The fruit of the Spirit is love, joy, peace, patience, kindness, goodness, faithfulness, gentleness and self-control.'"

"Hold it," Max said. "Let me write those down."

Nelson repeated, "'The fruit of the Spirit is love, joy, peace—'"

"A little slower."

He took a breath and quoted the words even slower as Max wrote them out at the bottom of the page.

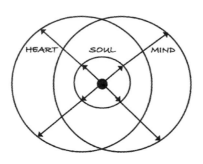

LOVE, JOY, PEACE, PATIENCE, KINDNESS, GOODNESS, FAITHFULNESS, GENTLENESS, SELF-CONTROL

We all stared at the paper.

Finally, Winona spoke, "That would be a wonderful way to live."

"But who can do it?" Joey said.

Max nodded, "Exactly. No one can. That's why they're called the fruit of the Spirit. Not the fruit of Joey, not the fruit of Winona, or the fruit of Max. They come from His Spirit. It's God doing His work inside us. Not us doing it, but God."

Nelson fired off another quote. "If a man remains in me and I in him, he will bear much fruit."

"So, all we must do is remain in Him," Winona said.

"Be still and know He's God," Joey quoted. Everyone nodded.

After a long moment, Winona finally summed it up. "It's like you've been saying. . .we just let God love us and love Him back."

And that's what our service is—just loving Him back by serving others.

All it takes is an act of our will. As I've said before, God has wired our house and supplied the electricity. All we have to do is be willing to flip the switch, and—*voila!*— His power and love flow through us.

And the deeper my circuitry is connected to Him, the more effective my service. I'm not saved by my service, I'm saved so I can serve. It may not always be easy, and it may be a sacrifice calling for Herculean faith. But if that service springs from the intimacy of Christ's presence, it will always be full of *His* joy. . .along with all the other fruit of *His* Spirit.

9

↔

A NEW WAY OF THINKING

Awhile ago I was in the back hills of Turkey researching for one of my earliest (and still one of my favorite) novels, *Fire of Heaven*. I was visiting each of the seven cities mentioned in the book of Revelation and waiting on the Lord for ideas. On one particular evening, I went down to a rural bazaar and struck up a conversation with a local shopkeeper. Somehow the topic of Jesus Christ rolled around (imagine that!), and eager to practice his debating skills, the man politely shredded my faith to pieces.

"You Christians," he said, shaking his head, "you make no sense."

"I'm sorry," I said. "What do you mean?"

"You are totally illogical. In Islam one plus one equals two. It will always equal two. You sin, you pay for it. It is a simple mathematical equation. But you, with your faith, there is no logic. With your faith, one plus one can equal anything."

I glanced up to see other shopkeepers gathering around. Apparently the village had no cable TV.

He continued, "You sin. . .nothing. You sin again. . .still nothing. A million plus a million and you still get zero. It makes no sense. Your faith is totally illogical."

My mind raced for an answer, but there was none. He had me and I had to come clean. "You're right," I said, "it's totally illogical. I guess when it comes to love, there is no logic."

He folded his arms and nodded. "And that, my friend, is

our difference. You refuse to think logically."

I nodded and saw a trace of disappointment in his eyes. (No doubt he was hoping for a worthier opponent.) The match was over before it began. But then another one of those out-of-the-blue thoughts came. By now we'd gathered quite a crowd, and common sense told me to keep my mouth shut. And since common sense has never been my high card, I said, "But I think we may have one other difference."

"And what is that?"

"Is God your Friend?"

"What? What did you say?"

I noticed his face growing strangely pink, but I felt a need to repeat, "Is God your Friend?"

"Such a thing is not possible." He was going from pink to red. "This is blasphemy!"

The quiet murmur from the crowd indicated he wasn't the only one who thought so.

"No one can be friends with God!" he sputtered. "Such a thing is blasphemy!"

I shrugged. "Well, I'm afraid that's another difference between us. God *is* my Friend."

"Blasphemy!" he repeated. *"Blasphemy!"*

And then, glancing at the other men's faces, a *not*-so-out-of-the-blue thought came. I thanked him for his time and got out of there as fast as I could.

I've never forgotten that encounter. Here was a man

who deeply revered his God, who prayed to him five times a day, who gave to the poor, who in some ways was a better servant than I ever was, and yet he didn't know the first thing about the God he was serving.

NOT A HISTORY LESSON. . .NOT A RELIGION

That is the difference between Jesus Christ and all other religious leaders. Only Jesus Christ spoke of a holy God who loved us more than His own life. A holy God who allows us to call Him "Abba." A holy God who takes so much pleasure in us that He actually rejoices over us in singing (see Zephaniah 3:17).

He calls us to a wedding feast where we rejoice and celebrate in His love for us and our love for Him. Yet how many times had I fooled myself into believing I had a relationship, when it was simply a well-structured philosophy? Or, since there's no other standard to compare it to, I had confined His love into a tidy religion. Both mind-sets stole from Christ's great glory. In the first, I had reduced Him to a historical teacher whose moral code I struggled to follow. In the second, I had turned Him into a religious taskmaster who kept score and was never satisfied.

How wrong both ideas were when compared with the real truth!

Folks from pastors to high school students tell me their

favorite novel of mine is *Eli*. It's a retelling of the gospel story as if it happened today in America, instead of 2,000 years ago. I wrote it to strip away the religious varnish I'd personally encased Jesus in, to take Him out of Sunday school picture books, and to remove all the cultural and historical insulation I hid behind so He'd be as fresh and revolutionary as the first time He showed up.

In secret, I wrote it for myself.

But by the letters I receive from readers saying it changed their lives, I'm guessing there are others whose faith has turned dry and religious or who have never fully grasped Christ's great love for them in the first place. My favorite letters are the ones saying, "I've been a Christian my whole life and now I finally get it."

Jesus Christ is more than some historical God trapped in the pages of the Bible. He is living, *now*. He is active, *now*. And He is committed to having a living, active relationship with His children as much *now* as He was back in the days when He walked the earth.

As far as God being a score-keeping, religious taskmaster? I have no doubt that when I die and stand before His throne, I'll be sobbing over all my failures and missed opportunities. And I'm just as sure that I'll hear that same tender voice I once heard in Rome say, "Get over yourself, friend. My Son, the one with the scarred body over there—He paid for it all. Now come up here and give your Dad a hug."

I'm looking forward to that day. It will be beyond joy.

But if I really believe in what Jesus did for me, it should be beyond joy *now*, because it's as real now as it will be then. Because God sees me that way *now*.

One of my favorite college students I mentored was trapped in a similar religious mind-set. He believed God loved him because He was obligated to, because it was in the new contract. But he just couldn't conceive of God actually *liking* him. Even on his best days, he would quote verses like, "All our righteous acts are like filthy rags" (Isaiah 64:6). (I shudder to think what he thought God felt about his worst days.) Try as he might, he just couldn't conceive of a God who really loved and rejoiced over him, which made it next to impossible for him to love and rejoice over God.

So one day, I asked him to grab a concordance and write down every verse in the Bible associated with joy. (Poor guy—there must be hundreds of them.) It really messed with his head, and to be honest I don't know if he ever completed the assignment. But the last time we spoke, he'd definitely grasped the concept in his mind. Now it was just a matter of it sinking into his heart.

SATURATED IN SPIRIT

There's a danger in books like this one, books that try to parcel up and separate how God works with each of us. He sees no division in His transforming work, no steps, no program. To Him, it's completely seamless. It's about one thing and one thing only: His passion for us. Even His insistence on our growing in holiness and loving others comes from His all-consuming love. And where love is found, or even the desire to be loved, there God will be, loving us and empowering us to love others.

I once wrote a movie script (and now a novella) titled *Supernatural Love*. It's the true story of Beth, a mother whose son was murdered in a drug deal that went sideways. Lewis, the killer, was eventually arrested and sentenced. Justice had been served.

But then the strangest thing happened. Several years later, Beth was in a prison auditorium waiting to visit someone when she heard the clear and unmistakable voice of the Lord saying, "Beth, the murderer of your son is in this room, and I want you to love him for Me."

As you can imagine, she put up quite a fuss—not only about hearing God's voice but about the request itself.

Finally, the voice gently asked, *"Beth, do you love Me?"*

She broke into tears. "Yes, Lord, You know I do."

"Then love Lewis for Me."

"But, Lord—"

"Daughter, do you love Me?"

"Lord," she sobbed, "You know I love You."

"Then love Lewis for Me."

"Please, Jesus, I, I—"

"Dear child, do you love Me?"

By now, she could only nod.

But the voice wasn't finished. *"Stand,"* was all He said.

Somehow Beth found the strength to rise to her feet.

"Now turn. Walk down the aisle."

Still sobbing, she obeyed, crying so hard she could barely see. After a dozen or so steps, the tender and gentle voice said, "Stop right here."

She did. And there was Lewis, sitting before her. She knelt down to him and, through her tears, blubbered out who she was. He freaked. Yet, somehow, before the authorities rushed in and dragged her away, she managed to say, "Jesus loves you. . .and so do I!"

And the oddest thing was, she really did. She couldn't explain it, but at that moment she felt an incredible rush of love for the lost young man—a love that, over the months, only grew.

She began writing him letters. He wrote back with mean, vindictive answers. But she didn't quit. She just kept on writing about Jesus and their love for him. Eventually, her family started calling her a traitor. Even her pastor told her she was getting carried away with all this love and forgiveness stuff. But she wouldn't stop. She continued reaching out to Lewis, sending him letter after letter.

Long story short, one day in solitary confinement, Lewis finally received Christ. After he wrote Beth and told her, she began taking ninety-minute bus rides from her hometown to visit him. And eventually, when they began talking to other hardened inmates about the forgiving love of Jesus Christ, the men listened—as evidenced by the dozens of Mother's Day cards she received from her brand-new sons in Christ.

My point? It was Christ's love that empowered Beth to obey. And it was Christ's love that achieved more good than a hundred Beths could have achieved through their own strength.

IN SUMMARY

Every fruit of the Spirit, every bit of devotion, service, and work must be an extension of God's love. To pursue them without His love is to push ahead under our own power. That would be as foolish as believing that the oil lamp wick we mentioned in the introduction could continue to burn for long without being saturated in oil. The wick would quickly burn itself up and become worthless ash.

When oil is mentioned in scripture, it often symbolizes God's Holy Spirit. If we are to be a light to the world, we must immerse ourselves in His Spirit. We must soak in Him. We must abide in His presence and drink deeply—so deeply that it's impossible for others to tell where we leave off and He begins. That is how we become the light that will change world.

Jesus tells us to "go into all the world and preach the

gospel to all creation" (Mark 16:15). But our efforts will be worthless if the good news of Christ's love and freedom shrinks back into the bad news of religion and slavery. We are commanded to share with others the abundant life Christ has given us. We are to share the abundance, not the dregs. Instead of some dried-up trickle that we squeeze out on our own, we are to share the "rivers of living water" that will "flow from within" (John 7:38). (Notice the verse says "rivers," not "river.")

Love, service, joy, sacrifice, and peace must all come from God first, from resting and abiding in His presence. God never asks for anything He hasn't already given us. And once we receive the abundance of His life and return it to Him through worship and through serving others, He receives it and returns it back to us in an even greater portion. Jesus put it this way: "Give, and it will be given to you. A good measure, pressed down, shaken together and running over, will be poured into your lap" (Luke 6:38).

When I'm saturated in Christ's love through adoring Him and being adored by Him, my desire to help others and tell them about His supernatural love grows even stronger. It's not forced; it's natural and organic. Often it even happens without words. It's as if the melody in my heart is so appealing that folks just naturally start asking for the lyrics.

When I focus first on deepening my relationship with Christ, even my prayers become more effective. They remind me that everything is a Father-son project in which I'm no longer praying *at* God, but praying *with* Him—or as a friend of mine says, "I'm no longer begging God as a widow, but asking as His bride. That's when love and works unite, flowing so strong and naturally that I can't tell the difference."

I remember being in the middle of the Northridge earthquake in 1994. It was a real ground shaker, and it killed dozens of people. Until then, I'd always thought of myself as one of the most selfish people on the planet. But as the house was rolling and dishes were falling out of our cupboards, I threw myself over our baby to save her life. And being the analytical writer I am, even then I remember thinking, *What? Are you nuts? Are you willing to give up your life to save hers?*

My answer was a resounding, *Wow! Will you look at this? Gee, I guess I am.*

That act of love, even though it meant risking my own life, was so spontaneous and natural that I was totally caught off guard. (And yes, I had the good sense to eventually scoop her up and run out of the house).

That's how it is with our Lord. Today my faith is more than theory. Today I would die for Him in a heartbeat (let alone serve however He asks). Not because I have to, not because I'm some great man of God, but because I'm so in love with Him that I can't help myself.

This is not a love manufactured through religion, programs, or works. It is a love that comes simply from abiding in God's presence. And from that abiding, I absorb His overwhelming passion for myself and for others—a passion so great that even when I try, I can't prevent it from overflowing and spilling out on the whole world.

Soli Deo gloria

OTHER BOOKS BY BILL MYERS

NOVELS

Angel of Wrath
Blood of Heaven
Child's Play
Eli
Fire of Heaven
Harbingers
Soul Tracker
The Face of God
The God Hater
The Judas Gospel
The Presence
The Seeing
The Voice
The Wager
Threshold
When the Last Leaf Falls

CHILDREN'S BOOKS

Baseball for Breakfast (picture book)
Blood Hounds, Inc. (mystery series)
Imager Chronicles (Bloodstone Chronicles) (fantasy series)
McGee and Me! (book/video series)
*Secret Agent Dingledorf and His Trusty Dog, Splat
(comedy series)*

The Bug Parables (picture book series)
The Elijah Project (suspense series)
The Incredible Worlds of Wally McDoogle (comedy series)
TJ and the Time Stumblers (comedy series)
Truth Seekers (action/comedy series)

Teen Books

The Dark Side of the Supernatural (nonfiction)
Faith Encounter (devotional)
Forbidden Doors (supernatural series)
Ancient Forces Collection
Dark Power Collection
Deadly Loyalty Collection
Invisible Terror Collection
Hot Topics, Tough Questions (nonfiction)

E-Book Series

Supernatural Love
Supernatural War

For a further list of Bill's books, sample chapters, and reviews, go to www.Billmyers.com

Or check out his Facebook page
www.facebook.com/billmyersauthor

DISCUSSION QUESTIONS FOR "THE JESUS EXPERIENCE"

CHAPTER ONE

What are the risks of always saying yes to God?

What are the benefits?

Why does God put us in situations over our heads?

How can we use those situations?

CHAPTER TWO

In all honesty, is God enough for you?

What leads us into putting the cart (serving) before the horse (adoring)?

How does spending time with God lessen our ability to serve?

How does it increase it?

CHAPTER THREE

What do you do to keep your love for God fresh and alive?

How does scripture do that?

Other than scripture, how do you hear God?

List five ways you express your adoration to Him?

CHAPTER FOUR

How have you seen Romans 8:28 apply in your own life?

How do we count something "pure joy" if we don't feel any joy?

Is praising God when we're feeling down hypocritical?

How would really believing Romans 8:28, James 1:2–4, and 1 Thessalonians 5:16–18 change your life?

CHAPTER FIVE

What can cause worship and adoration to be difficult?

What do we do during those times?

Have you seen the power of God released through worship?

Why is God's silence so important?

CHAPTER SIX

In what ways are you "stuck at the cross"?

How does "false humility" show up in your relationship to God?

Is relying on Christ's power to overcome our failures a cop-out?

What specific things does "the accuser" accuse you of?

How can you silence him?

CHAPTER SEVEN

If Christ has forgiven me of all sin, why obey?

How do I use Jesus to overcome sin?

How does judging myself cause me to judge others?

Think of a specific time of discipline. What did you feel?

In what ways are you grateful for it now?

CHAPTER EIGHT

What type of good fruit is born without God?

How is fruit born by the Holy Spirit different than fruit born through our own efforts?

How do we grow His fruit in our lives?

Is it possible to have deep, abiding faith without works?

CHAPTER NINE

How is Christianity different from other religions?

What ways do you personally stay saturated in the oil of God's Spirit?

What ways have you been pulled out of His oil and burned yourself out?

Can good works also pull us out of His presence?

What concepts in this book will remain with you?